DANIEL MEYER

Kentucky Haunts

Schiffer Publishing Ltd®

4880 Lower Valley Road • Atglen, PA 19310

Other Schiffer Books on Related Subjects:

Campfire Tales: Kentucky. Roberta Simpson Brown. Photographs by Thomas Lee Freese
ISBN: 978-0-7643-4231-8

Kentucky Spirits Undistilled. Lisa Westmoreland-Doherty
ISBN: 978-0-7643-3142-8

Strange Kentucky Monsters. Michael Newton
ISBN: 978-0-7643-3440-5

Designed by Molly Shields
Cover design by Matt Goodman
All photographs by the author unless otherwise noted.
Cheap hotel with a sign where the "T" is missing © alderd. Courtesy www.bigstockphoto.com.

Type set in Disgusting Behavior/Times New Roman

ISBN: 978-0-7643-5570-7
Printed in the United States of America

Published by Schiffer Publishing, Ltd.
4880 Lower Valley Road
Atglen, PA 19310
Phone: (610) 593-1777; Fax: (610) 593-2002
E-mail: Info@schifferbooks.com
Web: www.schifferbooks.com

For our complete selection of fine books on this and related subjects, please visit our website at www.schifferbooks.com. You may also write for a free catalog.

Schiffer Publishing's titles are available at special discounts for bulk purchases for sales promotions or premiums. Special editions, including personalized covers, corporate imprints, and excerpts, can be created in large quantities for special needs. For more information, contact the publisher.

We are always looking for people to write books on new and related subjects. If you have an idea for a book, please contact us at proposals@schifferbooks.com.

To all those haunted.
A special thanks to Alison and Chris
for sharing the journey.

Contents

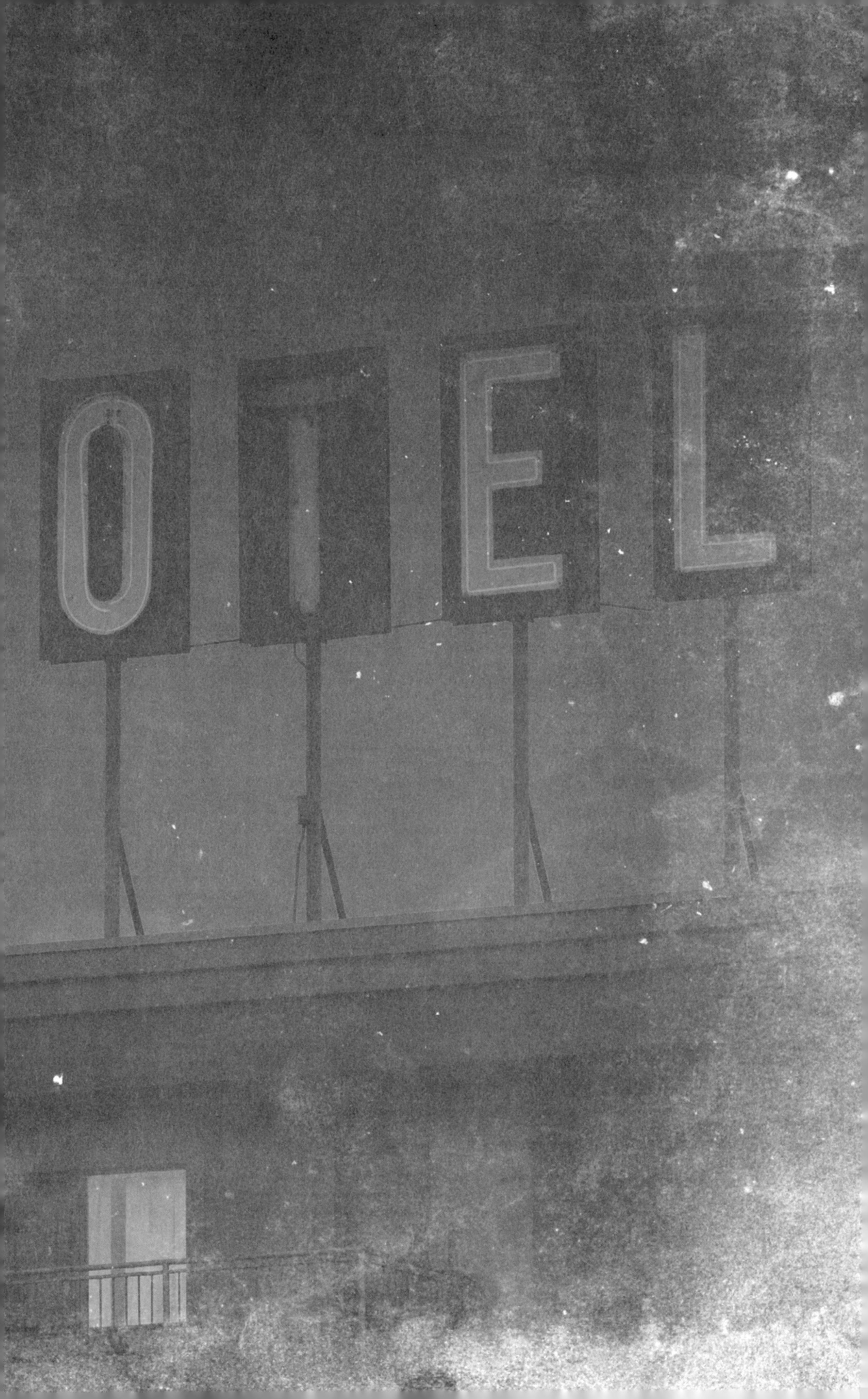
OTEL

Acknowledgments

In a book on the subject of ghosts, my first thanks goes to the spirits themselves; they made everything possible, and the plausibility (to the skeptic) or probability (to the believer) of their existence gives hope to us all when our time seems brief on this earthly plane.

I next want to thank all the managers, owners, and workers who share space with our cast of spirits—may you have many more experiences . . . each more satisfying than the one before.

Thanks to my editor at Schiffer Books—Dinah Roseberry—for her support, ideas, and easy-going nature. It was a pleasure to work with you.

Last, but certainly not least, thanks to my son, Christopher Meyer, and my friend, Alison Gale Porter, for sharing many of my journeys—as they say . . . it's the journey and not the destination that truly matter.

And, as always, thanks to you—the reader. Enjoy!

Spirits of the Dead
—Edgar Allan Poe

Thy soul shall find itself alone
'Mid dark thoughts of the gray
tombstone—
Not one, of all the crowd, to pry
Into thine hour of secrecy.

Be silent in that solitude,
Which is not loneliness—for then
The spirits of the dead who stood
In life before thee are again
In death around thee—and their will
Shall overshadow thee: be still.

The night, tho' clear, shall frown—
And the stars shall look not down
From their high thrones in the
heaven,
With light like Hope to mortals
given—
But their red orbs, without beam,
To thy weariness shall seem

As a burning and a fever
Which would cling to thee forever.
Now are thoughts thou shalt not
banish,
Now are visions ne'er to vanish;
From thy spirit shall they pass
No more—like dew-drop from the
grass.

The breeze—the breath of God—is
still—
And the mist upon the hill,
Shadowy—shadowy—yet unbroken,
Is a symbol and a token—
How it hangs upon the trees,
A mystery of mysteries!

Introduction

Those of us who have experienced ghosts and hauntings firsthand never forget those experiences. Indeed, our lives become running tallies of our moments with visitations from apparitions, the rappings on walls that are no longer there, the rappings on existing walls by unseen hands, the footsteps, the voices . . . We research the history of locations where ghosts have been seen, and we search for places where ghosts are known to visit. Once you have been blessed by a visit from the other side, well, there's no going back. It profoundly changes a person.

Kentucky is rich both in history and folklore, and its long tradition of storytelling has elements of both. Tales of the paranormal and hauntings are as popular today as they have been in centuries past. Think of Shakespeare's *Hamlet* and *Macbeth*. Think of Dickens's *A Christmas Carol*. Think of Casper! If ghosts are so much a part of our imagination, then surely that inspiration comes from something in the world around us. We may talk of recent ghosts or hauntings of historical figures as we dine in old houses converted into restaurants, between bites of fried chicken and mustard greens, or baked salmon and flame-teased asparagus, especially if the structure we dine in has a ghostly feel about it. Whether it's stories of Abraham Lincoln dreaming of his own assassination or of George Rogers Clark thrusting his riding crop into the ground so that a mighty cypress tree could live and grow to this very day, Kentuckians continue to enjoy sharing traditions and stories with family and friends, especially while sharing meals, or sleeping in historic inns, or traveling roadways through ancient countrysides, or even while visiting parks and historical monuments. Such stories of Abraham Lincoln and George Rogers Clark have several things in common. They both are important historical figures that helped make Kentucky what it is today, they both have ghost stories connected to them here in the commonwealth, and they both lived, slept, traveled, and broke bread in our fine state.

As towns grew into cities, early settlers continued to share tales and stories around the fireplace and dinner table throughout the eighteenth, nineteenth, and twentieth centuries. Midway through the twentieth century, entrepreneurs began to convert larger houses and buildings into restaurants or now-historic inns where people would continue to sleep, dine, and share stories with family and friends. And many of these houses, dating back to the late 1800s or earlier, had numerous folks who lived and died within those walls, so that ghosts and ghost stories began to share that space with overnight guests or diners. Thus, to this day, Kentucky's long tradition of traveling, breaking bread, and sharing that rich oral tradition of storytelling continues. Kentuckians will always enjoy traveling the commonwealth, exploring historic parks and inns, and sharing good food with family and friends, and they will always enjoy sharing a good ghost story.

This book will visit five facets of life in the commonwealth where ghostly happenings also occur

1. Haunted restaurants,
2. Haunted inns and hotels,
3. Haunted parks and natural areas,
4. Haunted roads and highways, and
5. Haunted cemeteries.

However, before we begin to travel, let's briefly explore what ghosts are and why they might visit the very same places we visit. Most people who might find interest in a book such as this already have preconceived notions on what ghosts are or what ghosts aren't. But for those of a skeptical nature—whom I like—and for those true believers—whom I like even more—here is an essay that delves a bit more deeply into the nature of ghosts.

Haunted

The dictionary defines "haunted" with three general meanings—all of which are all usually viewed as something less than positive. I offer a fourth that is quite positive.

1. The first, which parallels my own definition, regards a home being inhabited or frequented by ghosts (most people view this negatively—are they warped?).

2. Second, preoccupied, as with an emotion, memory, or idea.

3. Third—disturbed, distressed, or worried.

4. Which brings me to my own definition for haunted: LOVED.

This is not the simplest of ideas, so please bear with me.

We exist in dimensions both of time and space, or should I say of times and spaces (plural). What was here a moment or an eon earlier may be gone when next we blink our eyes or the stars above fade from being. Do we return once, or never, or return as waves to the shore as slaves of the tides?

And what of places? Are places as they seem, or does time alter their existence? As two sentient beings gaze at a single location, is it actually the same, independent of subjective thought and reasoning, or do different planes of existence alter spatial reality into two or more separate modes of being?

Such ponderings of time and space are meant as exercises related to life and death and, ultimately, to the haunting of dwellings. It has been suggested that a life that has been abruptly or tragically, even violently, cut short may imprint a life force or energy signature onto a certain physical location and may even cross the boundaries of time so as to repeat an energetic appearance linked to a physical space in what is referred to as a "residual haunting."

Most living creatures tend to be communal and live and breed with creatures of their own kin. Life is easier within a society where others care. A house is built, then another. And these dwellings that shelter us are, in turn, nested within a larger, natural setting. Houses stand against a background of trees filled with life and sound and meaning—squirrels bound and scamper, birds (beautifully colored with their blues, yellows, greens, golds, blacks, and reds) flitter and sing melodies and harmonies, insects sing and screech and scream and crawl and fly and creep. The trees themselves are alive and growing . . . green turning brown only to be reborn with virgin greenery hundreds, even thousands, of times; branches bend in the wind and strain to reach the moon at night and the sun by day.

And the natural backdrop of trees is also a foreground to the sky—deep and wide without end—clouds dripping rain or thundering with blasts of electric light . . . clouds blocking sun and moon or creating wispy veils of framework for a thousand pinpoints of life-giving heat an impossible distance away. The sky lives in its own right.

Set within the background of forest and sky, or clustered within a community of similarly cared-for structures, houses are designed to be a part (not apart) so that wood and stone and glass breathe life into a house to become a home. Thus, a house filled with creations crafted and nurtured by decades or centuries or eons is fully alive while it is loved and lived in and never truly dies until these lifetimes of collected memories have been totally obliterated. In fact, when such objects have been starved of attention and care, it may trigger an inbred reaction like a drowning sailor desperately gasping for air and breaking the surface of the water with frantic hands before sinking beneath the unforgiving waves of the ocean.

Within industrial-based societies such as ours, modern houses use building materials that are usually mass produced and are formed from petroleum-based products—plastics, composite metals, or other synthetic materials. However, there was once a time when "living" materials were used, such as wood and stone. And there was a time when a person was what he did. Master woodcarvers or stonemasons apprenticed under the vigilance of craftsmen who in turn trained before the experienced eyes of other craftsmen. Fathers taught sons, and those sons taught their sons, so that wood and stone came alive in the hands of artisans whose life's blood was revealed through their work. A mantelpiece or table was a product of love and dedication as hands and sweat and tool carved more than art—but life. A mantel comes to life when crafted by an artisan and then placed in a home where lords and ladies further lend life to such an object through years of love and admiration.

With the progression of time, technology also increased, as did the transient nature of homeowners. In decades and centuries past, more homes were retained by families, and those families in turn spent more time inside the home. More time within a dwelling also meant more time spent "communing" with objects—using them, caring for them, admiring them . . . "loving" them. A sense of connection was established with items such as desks, washing vessels, mirrors, service settings, chandeliers, books, records, artwork, quilts, chairs, tables, beds, curtains, and especially photographs in frames and portraits hung on walls as a place of honor, with traditions spanning generations. Such "items" were looked at lovingly for decades, even centuries.

Following this line of logic, places, and sometimes things, of antiquity are not so much haunted . . . as loved . . . loved by energies different than those as defined by mere vessels of flesh and blood . . .

Enter change.

A death, or many deaths spanning generations—these circumstances may leave a home longing for the love it once housed. And, in turn, souls that have passed on may long for the comfort and security a space once offered. "Progress" often strips a dwelling of its integrity . . . its classic lines of stone and wood traded without permission for plastics and mass-produced bric-a-brac during a renovation. Forests are often leveled to make room for progress and cookie-cutter houses that are devoid of style and character.

More change.

Poets and philosophers and theologians have long debated and have given countless sermons on everlasting love, the eternal life of the soul, and the existence of life after "death." Love of person—love of space. Connections. Time. Space. Love. Life. Death. Not all of these necessarily need to be eternal to be long lasting. They are all connections . . . bridges.

Death is change, but not necessarily an end.

Does death stop love and life from connecting two persons to one another, or persons from a loved space? Perhaps decades and centuries of actions and connections filled with strong emotions—hopes, dreams, longings, fears, disappointments, triumphs, passions, lusts, desires—bind life to time and space after death so that actions, entities, and souls still linger.

Consider more change.

New circumstances often bring eyes and lives that are detached from their newfound physical surroundings into a dwelling that was once loved, so that old "treasures" and places are now viewed as just things by the new inhabitants. Will these new sets of eyes "see" the love contained within the items or "see" the souls that connect time and space and life as they continue to dwell among a loved space in a type of temporal displacement? Usually not. Such connections of past to present may have the dead still viewing the dead as "alive" and the alive as intruders or annoyances, whereas the living are often blind to the past as they attempt to create a present and future for themselves.

Intelligent apparitions (as opposed to residual hauntings) may manifest themselves in a "need" to be seen . . . to be recognized, and it is only those persons who accept the past who can sense the "dead."

Ceremony and tradition have found the need to entomb the dead into coffins or caskets, mausoleums or pyramids, or even urns filled with desiccated ash and bone. All of these containers are "homes" for corpses. Imagine how much stronger the life force of living souls captured willingly within the walls of a house once called a home must be. Such a house, after the passing of its inhabitants, becomes a larger tomb for memories of not just one, but usually of many souls. Combine this collection of memories with the actual death within a house of the home's owner. How can such a dwelling not be loved or . . . haunted? And, on rare occasions, an owner's death, either on purpose or maliciously, becomes interred within the boundaries of the dwelling or nearby property. Time, space, life, death—are there distinct boundaries?

Are there haunted houses?

Perhaps.

Are there beloved homes?

Surely.

So, I ask again . . . are there haunted houses?

Most likely.

Close your eyes. Picture your home in your mind. Take your time so it is vivid and clear. Is this the house or apartment in which you currently live? Or did your mind and heart take you back to a childhood home or favorite house of long ago? Are you already haunting a house long before you are even dead? You wouldn't be the only one.

If the house (and home) you just envisioned is your current dwelling— congratulations! And if this home is multigenerational—more congratulations! Your house may be, or have been, haunted both by the living and the dead for many, many years.

To that image in your mind that you created a few moments before, flesh in some details regardless of how long it's been since you last physically set foot inside. Add the colors, the textures, the smells, the sounds. Was there a mantel, a fireplace, a favorite chair that your father sat in, a chandelier that set your eyes to sparkle as a child, a stove where your mother prepared enough meals to feed an army and often did every Thanksgiving and wedding day? Did you fall and chip or lose a tooth? Did you hide from your older sister or brother in a secret hideaway? Did you sneak away to the attic or rooftop or beneath the stairs to read? Did you learn to appreciate music at the bench of the piano or learn to dance at the turn of a knob to the radio or record player? Does a certain song come to mind? Did you play dress up? Did you rehearse lines for a school play? Did you receive or give your first kiss somewhere in the house? Can you feel a thousand good-night hugs? Can you smell Sunday morning breakfast . . . the muffins . . . the bacon . . . the coffee? Can you hear your pet's nails echo through the hall? Can you feel the give of the mattress as your dog or cat climbs into bed with you? Did you receive spankings for not doing homework or for sassing your parents? Did your mother or father die on a winter's morn in his or her bed?

Did YOU die there?

Is this house haunted by the living, or the dead, or both?

In closing, I offer you this blessing—may your love never die and may your house forever be haunted!

—Daniel Meyer

Ghostly Experience

If we let ourselves believe, most of us have experienced something that we can't explain. For me—I have been visited my entire life and realized early on that I was a sensitive, or one who is able to detect beings from the spiritual realm. Sometimes I can communicate directly, sometimes I merely feel emotions—usually confusion, loneliness, or sadness, while at other times I sense only a persistent and urgent calling such as, "I'm here, I'm here, I'm here," or "Look at me, Look at me!" Imagine if you were surrounded by people who ignored you for a long length of time, not because they wanted to, but because they merely didn't know you were there. And then, in walks someone they know can see them or hear them. BINGO! The "haunting" intensifies so that it is more than just a creak on the stairs or "misplaced" keys.

I will relate here three of my past experiences that "prove" that ghosts exist. At least in my mind they are real. You may remain skeptical or need to see for yourself.

For a couple of years, I shared a living space in the basement apartment of a house built at the turn of the twentieth century. The walls were large stones. The windows let in little natural lighting. And from the moment I stepped inside, I was "greeted" by the spirit of a motherly young woman and a tremendously lonely and shy boy. They were not related. I felt that the young woman stayed to console the child . . . to ease his loneliness. A dog and a cat, my girlfriend's, shared this space. They watched along with me as the woman—the gray lady as I came to know her—would pass from the hallway or bathroom to the bedroom. That was always her path. Their heads would follow her along with mine, but my girlfriend never saw a thing. Sometimes the gray lady would quickly take a few steps so that it was a quick turn of your head that was required, while other times she would walk slowly, and the pets would stare as if they were half-expecting a treat or a rub on the head.

My most vivid encounter was while I was sitting on the toilet in the early dawn. I kept the door open because it creaked, and I didn't want to disturb my girlfriend's slumber (I would flush when she awoke!). The diffused light let me make out shapes but not the fine detail that we see in the bright light of day. I was wide awake. Once I awaken, there is no returning to sleep. That is my curse and my blessing. As I sat, I watched the gray lady approach from the bedroom. She appeared to float just above the floor as if she were shuffling her feet rather than striding. I did not see her feet. She stood not ten feet away. She slowly turned her head to "look" at me and then slowly looked away once more toward the corner of the bedroom where I always felt the presence of the little boy. She then returned to the bedroom, gliding slowly until she was no longer in sight. My girlfriend would soon walk the same path. Their size and shape were totally different. Their "walks" were also different. You recognize the one you love by the sound of her footsteps, the position of her head, her essence! These were two separate women. And they both *were*!

At around the same time, I went to a tragic funeral of a friend of a friend. It was a closed-casket funeral due to the graphic nature of the death. I had never met or even seen the deceased. I was there for moral support and out of respect. I sat in the second row. While eulogies were given, I saw from the corner of my eye a figure sitting in a closed balcony section. When I looked directly at the young man, he was gone. I could not view him directly. He had longish wavy hair and gray eyes. In the same way we sense emotion, we can also communicate with mental directives and questions. I asked for a sign that he wanted to speak to me. I mentally pictured the moving of a nearby plant's leaves as a method of proof. As I grasped the mental image, the lamp by the plant instantly flickered. I asked for him to repeat the action. He did so.

I proceeded to ask a series of questions at different time intervals—ten seconds, twenty seconds, a minute ten seconds. With each question came an immediate flicker—once for yes, twice for no. The content of the conversation shall remain private to protect the family of the deceased. After the service concluded, I walked over to inspect the lamp. The bulb was secure in its socket. The switch was tight and functioned properly. The plug was firmly placed in the wall. The lamp turned on and off with no flickering whatsoever. I described the visitor in the balcony to a friend, and she confirmed it was the deceased. I also found photos that I had not yet seen and confirmed for myself. I spoke with the dead on that day. You won't convince me otherwise.

And lastly, I will include another story from my own house. My home at the time had been built in the 1950s, not particularly old, and I had frequently heard footsteps walking down the hall for several years. However, the footsteps never entered my bedroom at the end of the hall. I often waited, I asked "her" to enter and talk, but she never did. One late night, I had fallen asleep on the couch and awoke thinking that I would return to bed before I needed to get up again for work. Unfortunately, I was wide awake and decided to wash a few dishes that I had neglected to do earlier in the evening. Once finished, I turned out the lights and headed for bed. My cat had reached the warmth of my bed before me. Smart girl! Then things changed from the ordinary. I turned out the bedroom light and rolled under the sheet and light cover—it was spring. Suddenly, my cat leaped from the bed, hit the floor with claws churning, and bolted all the way down the hall until she reached the living room at the far end of the house. As I heard her skid to a stop, I felt the mattress sink down on the opposite side of the bed. The mattress continued to move as if someone was rolling toward the middle, until I felt someone or something snuggle against the small of my back. This pressure was far larger than my easily alarmed cat! I have had spectral encounters for all of my life, as stated earlier, so I was far from concerned. I merely pulled the sheet tighter since I wasn't sure if my visitor was a cover hog, and closed my eyes for sleep. I felt no danger and was, therefore, comfortable with the situation. My cat would be required to find shelter elsewhere if only for the night.

Okay—after reading my experiences with the other side, you may not yet be convinced, and that is fine. That is not my goal. I merely want you to know my level of experience and ability. I have had many other experiences— many of which I include on the pages that follow. How about you decide for yourself by joining me as we visit a plethora of haunted locations across the commonwealth of Kentucky?

It is always best to rule out natural phenomena when considering whether or not a place is haunted, and never believe a facility is haunted merely because of stories (mine included!); however, also never discount your instincts and always keep an open mind. Now, with that said . . . let's explore some Kentucky Haunts! First up—let's find something good to eat.

"Being dead does have its advantages."
—Dana Michelle Burnett, *Spiritus*

CHAPTER ONE

Haunted Restaurants

Eating among good company is one of the greatest pleasures in life. And what better company is there than ghosts? I spend a great deal of time in restaurants both as a diner and in a professional position. I am afforded an inside look at the daily operations of many of Kentucky's finest restaurants and have the great honor to call many restaurant owners and managers by the title of friend. I often visit restaurants before they are open to the public, and I explore the facilities intimately from the cellar to the attic, and it is during these times that I often "introduce" new owners to their new ghost friends. By contrast, other restaurants have been haunted for a very long time, with legends and stories circulating far and wide.

Many of Kentucky's restaurants were once private homes where a great deal of effort and expense has gone to convert them to a new life of food service. It is these stately old structures that have also provided a haven for the departed. Not only have I sensed many ghostly presences, but I have seen objects move before my eyes and even had equipment with new batteries become instantly drained as I've entered darkened cellars or attics. Let me state right here that all the restaurants to follow are safe eateries . . . no murders have taken place at any of these establishments (well, not for a very long time), and no one is hurt or attacked by anyone or anything natural or supernatural (unless posted warnings exist here and at the restaurant). With that said, let's travel across the great state of Kentucky in search of some good food . . . and some ghosts!

Some locations, whether they are cities or forests, are more haunted than others. Compare the Tower of London with a miniature golf course, or the battlefields of Gettysburg with your local playground, and you will obviously note the differences not only in the histories of the places, but in the "feel" of the places. When traveling and looking for places with a spirited past—and present—sometimes you just get lucky. That's how it was with Paducah, Kentucky. For a town with a population of approximately 25,000, there were more ghost stories and haunted locations than you could throw a spirit stick at! There had even been witch burnings down by the river many moons ago—what better way to spend a Saturday night!

Just into town, my son and I walked into Wildhair Studio's Rock Shop (in the process of relocating at the time of our visit, but check their website for their new location: www.nicerockshop.com) and could immediately feel the haunted history of the location. Inside the first doorway we entered in Paducah, the past was opened up to us. It seemed the young daughter of the building's long-passed owner once liked to watch the yearly parade as it passed by the front window. Therefore, placing a locked door between the front window and the deceased owner's office, where the little girl would stay out of mischief, resulted not only in the disappointment of the ghostly girl, but also in multiple broken locks for the new owners until an understanding was reached. The rock shop's owner, Susan Edwards, was also kind enough to share not only ghost stories, but also stories and photos of frequent fairy activity in Paducah and beyond. In addition, she pointed us in the direction of local historians and the guide of the local ghost tour that takes place every October. And one last thing . . . she asked if we were aware of the place we were headed next.

Shandies Restaurant

Many businesses and restaurants have shared the space between the walls, floors, and ceilings of the C. C. Cohen Building, built around 1865, including a clothing store, a dry goods store, and, in 1914, the R. L. Peacher Liquor Dealers and the Rehkopf Distilling Company. The Cohen family owned this prime corner, now listed as 202 Broadway, from around 1921 until 1980, when the last member of the Cohen family, Stella Cohen Peine, died upstairs in her apartment. For many years it was open as a beautiful restaurant known as C. C. Cohen's.[1] As of this writing, it is under new ownership and is called Shandies.

Since Stella's departure from this world, restaurant workers, as well as guests, have reported many strange occurrences that they attribute to Stella, such as chairs mysteriously moving by themselves, salt and pepper shakers tipping over, lights flickering, cold spots, strange movements in mirrors and

Fig. 1: C. C. Cohen Building, Paducah,
home of Shandies Restaurant.

brass, and even glasses falling from parts of the bar. Even more people claim to have seen Stella peering out an upstairs window in an area that has been used only for storage.

While dining, I asked the friendly and capable server if she had witnessed anything unexplainable. She reported that she had worked there only a few months, but when she had just started, a fellow worker had told her of a young girl customer inquiring about a woman staring down from the second floor. The second floor was unused at the time, and, of course, the woman who had been sighted was no longer visible. Another Stella sighting?

The food, by the way, was also out of this world. I had a meatloaf sandwich and orange-braised asparagus with an ice-cold Corona (or two), while my son had a very large burger and some of the best mac 'n' cheese ever to find space on a fork!

Fig. 2: Shandies Restaurant, Paducah. These are the stairs leading to upper floors where Stella has been sighted.

Just inside the entrance to Shandies there is a staircase that gives a taste of the days gone by. Obvious in the photo is one of the many bricked-up doorways that speak of one of the building's many changes over the past century and a half. Often, you will hear stories that report such changes as being unappreciated by spirits, since they tend to enjoy their home staying the same year after year after year. Enjoy great food in a great atmosphere? Try making Shandies in Paducah a regular haunt of yours!

Boone Tavern
Berea

Berea, in Madison County, is best known for its art festivals, for its historic restaurants and buildings, and as the home to Berea College, a private, liberal arts college. This small town of just over 14,000 is also home to Historic Boone Tavern, opened in 1909, to house guests of the college. It was named for Kentucky explorer Daniel Boone, who frequently slept at nearby Fort Boonesborough. The "Tavern" part of the name derives from the historical definition, which refers to a public inn for travelers, rather than from the modern definition, related to the sale of alcoholic beverages. The hotel's hospitality extends far beyond providing rest for weary travelers; its restaurant features legendary cornbread soufflé locally known as Boone Tavern Spoonbread, among other mouth-watering original dishes that include regional Kentucky Proud ingredients.

Construction of Boone Tavern began in 1907 and was based on designs by the New York architectural firm of Cady & See. The building was built with bricks manufactured by students in the college's brickyard, and was constructed by the college's Woodwork Department at a total cost of $20,000. In 2008, the hotel underwent a $9.6 million renovation. Although ghostly activity had been reported since the early 1900s, spectral activities increased after the renovation.

The ghostly happenings occur on all floors both in the hotel and the restaurant. I chose to include it here in the restaurant chapter due to the occurrence of some favorite pranks played by the ghost of an overly active little boy. Several workers have reported an ice scoop shooting off the top of the ice machine in the restaurant's kitchen. Utensils are also frequently moved in the restaurant areas. Many staff members speak to the little boy, and all claim that he is playful and active but never mean in any way. The child's laughter and footsteps have been heard by workers and guests alike throughout the restaurant and hotel. The apparitions of the boy and what may be his mother or at least a woman acting in a motherly manner have been witnessed by many, especially on the upper floors of the hotel, including in rooms 303 and 312.[2] A separate apparition that appears in photographs is that of a young black boy. While waiting for my table (even ghost writers have to wait their turn!), I felt drawn to the stairs leading to the upper floors.

Are you in the mood for some fine dining and a comfortable bed in a historic hotel in central Kentucky? You may make a new friend overnight!

Fig. 3: Boone Tavern, Berea.

Jailhouse Pizza
Brandenburg

Meade County offers a restaurant with excellent food, outstanding history, beautiful views of the Ohio River, and, if that weren't enough, ghostly visitors on what seems to be a regular basis. What is currently Jailhouse Pizza was once the Meade County Jail, built in 1906. The red-brick building functioned as a jail until the mid-1970s, served several functions through the final decades of the twentieth century, and was purchased by its current owner, Kevin Stich, in 2010. Although some portions of the building have been modified to cook and serve pizza, salads, wings, and a delicious mix of Italian favorites, most of the structure remains true to its former design and function. There are jail cells (with tables) and even a trap door on the second floor, where hangings once occurred. A couple of the more notable former inmates include Hank Williams Sr. and John Hunt Morgan of the "Morgan Raiders." Frank and Jesse James were guests of the old Meade County Jail nearby on Main Street, which was operating during the 1800s.

The operators of Jailhouse Pizza are proud both of the historical and paranormal aspects of the restaurant—as they should be! The following is taken directly from their menu:

> History is alive and well in these walls. We are known to have some inmates that have decided to serve a sentence longer than life. One that has been named Bigsby, has been known to roam the jail still. From time to time you might see, hear, or maybe even feel things that cannot be explained. If you do experience something, please let us know. We love to hear stories of what our more permanent patrons are up to. In the meantime be sure to walk around and soak in all the natural and sometimes supernatural history around our restaurant.

Some of the reported ghostly activity includes footsteps upstairs, the slamming of heavy cell doors when no one is present, missing items in the kitchen, pulled hair, spilled drinks and rearranged food items (as reported by customers), shadow figures, and voices that frequently call your name. A number of ghost investigations have been conducted here, including by *Oddity Files* and the Dark Side of Louisville Paranormal Society. In fact, the restaurant offers groups the opportunity to conduct investigations after business hours.[3] Check their website for prices and availability at www.jailhousepizza.com.

Whether you are hungry, enjoy history, enjoy the company of spirits, or all of the above—this is the place to be!

Bobby Mackey's Music World
Wilder

Although more a music hall than a restaurant, no book on Kentucky's haunted locations would be complete without mentioning Bobby Mackey's in northern Kentucky. When I mentioned earlier that no one is ever hurt in any of the establishments unless noted otherwise—well, here is the disclaimer that is posted at the entrance to Bobby Mackey's:

> Warning to our patrons: This establishment is purported to be haunted. Management is not responsible and cannot be held liable for any actions of any ghosts/spirits on this premises.

And if that is not clear, the late Peter D. Moscow, PhD, MDS Rad, past president of the United States Psychotronics Association, had this to say: "I have never encountered a more malevolent or destructive case than that which I experienced at Bobby Mackey's Music World in Wilder, Kentucky."

Here's a brief history of the property. Built in the 1850s, what is currently known as Bobby Mackey's originally served as a slaughterhouse and meat-packing operation. The only remaining feature of the original building is the well in the basement, where blood and refuse were drained from the animals. The slaughterhouse closed in the early 1890s. According to local lore, the abandoned basement soon became a ritual site for occultists, and the well was used to dispose of the butchered animals used during their ceremonies. From the 1930s through the 1950s, the building functioned as a casino, operating as Buck Brady's Primrose Club in the early 1940s. After renaming the facility "The Latin Quarter," it flourished until 1961, when law authorities began to get tough on organized crime. After that, several businesses quickly moved in and out of the location. The particularly rough "Hard Rock Café" opened in 1970 but was closed in 1977, after several bouts of gunplay. Bobby Mackey's Music World opened in 1978.[4]

The ghostly activities at this popular music hall revolve around two tragic female figures. A young woman, Pearl Bryan, was murdered and allegedly decapitated, with the two men who cut her life short staying behind to haunt the place where they disposed of her head—down a floor drain that led to the old well, in what some claim was a satanic sacrifice. Decades after the murder, the well was once more uncovered by a caretaker who unknowingly opened a "portal to hell." This same caretaker soon claimed to be possessed by an entity freed from the portal.

Bobby Mackey's Music World now promotes haunted tours of the basement and other areas, with the well, as described on their website, "a legendary location of occult activity."

During the nightclub days there were dressing rooms for performers down in this basement. Johanna, a club dancer from the 1940s, fell in love with a man whom her mobster father did not approve of. The same caretaker who uncovered the cursed well and became possessed also found her diary that described her sad tale. The mob murdered her suitor, and she soon thereafter poisoned herself in her dressing room. A final love poem was scrawled on the basement wall.

Many visitors have reported physical and emotional attacks at Mackey's, including his late wife, Janet, who claimed she was assaulted by an invisible entity. Others have claimed they have been attacked by forces that tossed them across the room. Employees, visitors, and paranormal investigators have documented or reported experiences with shadow figures, disembodied voices, unexplainable mists, balls of light, feelings of other beings present, and electronic voice phenomena (EVPs). Some claim that as many as forty different spirits may inhabit the site. The dark entity that was released when the portal was opened is said to be particularly dangerous to women.[5] This synopsis of the haunted activity was summarized in a recent article by the website www.doubtfulnews.com.

Obviously there are strong believers as well as skeptics regarding this location, and that's how it should be. Only by being skeptical can we discover the truth. If you're in northern Kentucky, find out for yourself at Bobby Mackey's Music World. However, be careful—you have been warned!

After roaming from town to town across the state, I will now take you to a selection of restaurants in my hometown of Louisville. Since I live here, and because it is by far the largest city in the commonwealth, it has disproportionately more restaurants and stories.

Highlands Tap Room Grill
Louisville

As mentioned, one of my favorite nonofficial roles during my day job is to gently introduce folks to the reality that they are sharing a space with a spirit or spirits. I do this as gently as possible . . . making such initial comments as, "Ever hear or see anything unusual here?" or "Do you or any of your staff ever experience things that you can't explain?" If they are not receptive to the subject, I quickly lead the conversation in another direction. However, if they are interested in hauntings or quickly begin to share experiences, I introduce them to my collected knowledge as a sensitive.

The Highlands Tap Room Grill is one such place. Located at 1056 Bardstown Road in the heart of the Highlands, this bar and grill is a converted residence that has retained energy and emotion from past residents. As I first toured the upstairs rooms, I felt the strong presence of an elderly woman. Most of the upstairs rooms are unfinished and used for storage, but I felt an insistent and constant pull. At the time, when they were just opening, few had recognized the happenings around them as ghostly experiences, but as time

Fig. 4: Highlands Tap Room Grill, Louisville. *Grossmutter* has been seen on these stairs many times.

went by, the staff began to hear their names called on occasion when no one was around, items would be moved, a touch was felt here and a tug at someone's hair was felt there, and even guests reported seeing an apparition on or near the stairs. Some pieces came falling into place when a former owner of the old residence visited and said his grandmother passed on upstairs. Many of the staff now refer to her as *Grossmutter*, which is the formal word for grandmother in German. When I learned of the new information, it felt good to see that my instincts and abilities were in tune.

This lively bar has excellent food, beer, and spirits (both kinds), in addition to live music, karaoke, billiards, and an outdoor patio. The owners and staff are friendly and attentive. I have enjoyed the food, as well as a cold brew on occasion, but my favorite part is the sensation of the past being revisited and shared.

Only staff go upstairs, but I feel every time, just beyond that door, that *Grossmutter* is somewhere between yesteryear and today.

Corbett's: An American Place
Louisville

Since its opening in December 2007, Corbett's has served some of the finest food in Kentucky. It is among a relative few to be awarded the AAA Four Diamond Award in addition to many other accolades, such as its inclusion on *Esquire*'s list of "Best New Restaurants of 2008." Their website nicely sums up their dedication to excellence:

> Corbett's features an inventive menu and cutting-edge technology, a stunning interior design, a menu with the highest quality ingredients, extensive wine list, impressive artisanal cheese selection and an interactive digital chef's table.

That's the now.

The then! Corbett's was formerly known as the Von Allmen mansion, built in 1850. This was the same year that President Zachary Taylor left office. It has even been rumored that this property was later acquired by Taylor as the settlement of a dispute. The twelfth president is interred just minutes away. The Von Allmen estate was the site of the first dairy farm in Kentucky and is surrounded by century-old maple and sweet bay magnolia trees. The mansion has magnificent architectural details: a grand staircase, fourteen-foot ceilings, an all-brick-and-limestone cellar, and gorgeous woodwork.[6]

Fig. 5: Corbett's: An American Place, Louisville.

Of course, Corbett's inclusion in this book is interesting in how the past interacts with the present. I walked through the mansion during its beautiful restoration as well as after it began serving meals. My immediate perception was of an insistent presence in the cellar, among the magnificent limestone walls and the dim lighting. On subsequent visits I was again drawn to this space. Several staff members expressed that they heard their name called when they were alone, felt slight touches, noticed items moved and replaced, and, most interestingly, observed the opening and spilling of "unopened" packages in the dry storage . . . located in the cellar. There are rooms for small gatherings in the cellar if you would like to dine in the company of curious spirits. But wherever you choose to dine here at Corbett's, it will be an outstanding evening.

Note: As this book went to press, Corbett's is now closed. Another victim of progress.

Captain's Quarters
Louisville

Captain's Quarters Riverside Grille offers delicious seafood dishes, international cuisine, and a selection of refined American fare—all served along the scenic banks of the Ohio River. This location has a lot of history going back to the turn of the nineteenth century. The following history lesson is adapted from the Captain's Quarters website on the "Our History" tab.

"Along the shore of the Ohio River where it meets Harrod's Creek, named for Colonel James Harrod, the old Harrod's Tavern once stood. Its first proprietor was one Captain Cavendar, who, realizing the need for a way station for weary river travelers, offered grog, conversation, and overnight lodging (in lean-tos nestled against the side of the building) to the procession of boatmen, adventurers and settlers who traveled this way."

This location was ideal since most river captains were loath to take the falls of the Ohio River during the night. Cargo was unloaded here and transported over the old Harrods Creek Road to Jeffersontown, Middletown, and the "settlement" of Louisville or, if going the other way, loaded here to find its way downstream or to points north via the ferry (rigged by the capable Captain Cavendar) across the river to Utica. The first developers of the Captain's Quarters site were drawn to the area due to the ferry between Utica, Indiana, and Harrods Creek. "The Lentz family, natives of Germany, had emigrated to Utica and Clark County from Pennsylvania shortly after the turn of the century, drawn to opportunities and quickly establishing themselves as successful millers and farmers. By operating the ferry between the two towns, the Lentzes secured an advantage over other mills."

The Lentz family began assembling land in the early 1840s and erected at least one building to house a tavern as well as other enterprises, such as a storehouse and docks. The Lentzes' businesses prospered along Harrods Creek for most of the nineteenth century. In 1890, the widow Mary Lentz Cavendar ended fifty years of family ownership when she finally sold the property.

Fig. 6: Captain's Quarters, Louisville. Dining area.

Fig. 7: Photo archive in Captain's Quarters showing the
extent of the 2011 flooding.

Few local examples of riverside architecture survive in any form from
before 1850. The Lentz Tavern, although greatly altered, is a graphic re-
minder of early settlement in Jefferson County and the Falls region, providing a unique look at life before trains and rapid industrialization.

The Captain's Quarters is dedicated to the proposition that camaraderie,
warmth, and hospitality live today within these old (and new) walls as surely
as it did when the sign outside read "Harrods Tavern."[7]

Thus, we have history, a great location, and delicious food and drink,
which finally brings us to spirits of another kind—ghosts. I talk to literally
thousands of individuals in the food industry, and a name that comes up over
and over is . . . Captain's Quarters. Reports of voices when the restaurant is
empty, touches, gentle tugs, and shadow figures are commonplace. And if I
had a dollar for every person who said his or her name was called . . .

However, the place has so much more than history; it also has tragedy
and disaster. Situated on the Ohio River, it is prone to periodic flooding.
Figure 6 shows the high watermark of the May 2, 2011, flood along the back
window, while Figure 7 provides documentation of the extent of the flooding.
Are the echoes here merely the lapping of spectral waters, or have people
drowned here over the centuries? It's a fantastic place to have a drink, grab

a bite to eat, watch the sun reflect off the water, and think of ghostly might-have-beens! Rank not required.

Derby City Antique Mall
Louisville

Louisville has a very special place—part shopping mecca, part distributer of hidden culinary wonders, and part portal to the past. The Derby City Antique Mall, located at 3819 Bardstown Road, has a café on the ground level. It caters to the mall's shoppers and has often changed names and operators since the mall opened in 1998. What hasn't changed is the large number of ghostly experiences that seem to happen on a regular basis.

The large red-brick building that currently sits shrouded in the shadow of mature trees was once called the Hikes Graded School and was built in 1927 as an independent public school for grades one to eight. Jefferson County Public Schools took charge in 1950 and maintained the structure until the school closed in 1975.[8]

With names such as Bluegrass Bistro, Bluegrass Café, and others, the hidden cafeteria has served many delicious dishes over the years. However, if you pause to think of the changes here over the many decades, my description of "haunted" that I used in the introduction is quite accurate. There's ample reason to believe that this building, and especially this dining area, retains spirit energy—whether residual or intelligent. I believe it has both. Think back to the school cafeteria that you dined in as a child. There's always a memory or two that stands out . . . sitting with friends in those important cliques that form, a few social loners by themselves, a bully or two spilling your milk or tripping smaller kids in line, the teacher's table in the front as they perch with that collective, watchful stare. That was then.

Now—there are pieces of antique furniture clustered in groups and pulled from various locations only to wait for an appreciative eye, bookcases stuffed with old periodicals and books with musty-smelling bindings, tables and glass cases overloaded with bric-a-brac. Yes, the cafeteria is completely different now—all the way down to the worn floor covering. However, the kitchen is nearly identical to the way it was when it functioned as the school kitchen. The same sinks and pipes and green-tiled walls remain. An old—not original—walk-in cooler is still there, although it hasn't functioned for decades and is now used for storage. There is a bare bulb with a pull-chain switch in the kitchen restroom that until very recently required a twist of the bulb to make the connection to turn the light on and off. There are a couple of small, dark rooms with odd-shaped doors, whose original functions have been lost to time.

The kitchen is a haven of how things used to be. The kitchen is also very haunted. Every café worker I have spoken to over the years has shared ghost stories—more than can be remembered at a single sitting, since they tend to accumulate like dust on a forgotten desk in an unused room. Joe and Sharon Ethington—owners of the Bluegrass Café from 2010 to 2015—would share a ghostly experience or three every time I came to visit. I truly miss our conversations—of good books, of warm meals, of ghostly visitors. I would always eat at a corner table next to an unused door by an old piano, with my back to the wall so I could watch the dining room. This dining area had also been changed extensively to serve guests rather than students. Many of the tales of unexplained happenings here fall in line with the possible spirit of a black custodian that liked to flirt. He was "conversed with" by a local ghost-hunting group that conducted an investigation at the antique mall. In this room, which seats about fifty diners, there are gentle touches, whispers or cool breaths at ear level, playful tugs at loose curls of hair, and subtle pinches to rounded bottoms—all directed toward women of course. My favorite occurrence was an earring tugged from an ear lobe to fall—not down to the floor as gravity would dictate—but at an angle to a nearby table.

The adjoining portion of the old cafeteria has stories as well. I am always drawn to a couple of antique hutches for sale and a corner where many books and a couple of gargoyles sit watching and waiting for someone to love them once more. I have been told that the paranormal investigators detected higher energy in these locations. I'm not surprised.

The kitchen has more familiar energies—names being called, the echo of a hello, an opening door, items removed and playfully returned, and, of course, just the feeling that someone else is near . . . but just out of sight.

More recently, a kitchen operator came and went within a very short span of time due in part to some very disturbing spectral visits. I have never felt such energies, but this operator felt compelled to place crucifixes above each door and entryway. The current entrance from the old cafeteria to the café dining area has a heavy latticework gate that is pulled together and locked nightly. On one occasion, the large and heavy cross that had been nailed above the entry was found broken and twisted on the inside of the locked gate upon arrival in the morning. Not a fan of crosses? Another café owner has arrived recently, in 2016, with more tales, but none as dark as this (that I am aware of).

Upstairs, on the second floor, I have experienced and been told of a residual haunting where the past meets the present. Here, there is an energy that walks from one "classroom," crossing the hall and entering into another "classroom." A teacher assisting a fellow teacher? A budding romance? This residual haunting is very different than dining with the ghosts downstairs.

Whether you are hungry or want to shop—there is much to be seen and "felt" at the Derby City Antique Mall. It is indeed one of my favorite places to travel back through time.

Louisville

A circle has 360 degrees symbolizing wholeness . . . completeness . . . some might say wellness—add friendly folks, reasonable prices, and a casual, eclectic atmosphere and you have Café 360—located at 1582 Bardstown Road in the heart of the Highlands in Louisville, Kentucky. There are also doors that open on their own, an occasional apparition, and a "stairway to nowhere," but we'll get to that soon enough.

Google Reviews describes Café 360 as a "quirky, 24/7 hangout offering strong drinks, pub-grub, and an extensive hookah selection in arty digs." This description is both concise and accurate. Their menu includes Middle

Fig. 8: Bar area in Café 360. There's a certain feel in the air.

Fig. 9: Café 360, Louisville.

Eastern / Mediterranean fare and American standards as well as vegan meals, soups, salads, and a variety of breakfast dishes. To get a feel . . . think Kentucky Hot Brown, pita delights, BBQ pork, grilled chicken sandwich, tuna melt, quesadilla, ravioli, fried catfish, beef strips, Szechuan pork, a Philly cheesesteak sandwich that barely fits on your plate (my personal favorite), omelets, and waffles. If you see a pattern other than variety . . . let me know. The staff is as friendly as any staff I have ever encountered, and personalities here are as interesting and favorably eccentric as the décor and neighborhood. There are pieces of artwork on the walls (by local artists, and for sale to the lucky buyer); graffiti in the restrooms; strong, cold drinks twenty-four hours a day; and lots of ghost stories from staff and customers.

During my many visits, I have felt the very strong presence of at least one spirit, especially in the second-floor area, which has been used for storage for a substantial chunk of time and is currently a hookah bar. And my feelings occurred before I knew anything of the building's history or heard any stories. After having such feelings, I inquired and, man overboard, did I hear stories! Off the upstairs hallway, there is a door leading to a wooden staircase to

Fig. 10: Stairway to nowhere, Café 360. The upper level has been torn away and these stairs lead to the ceiling on the top floor.

nowhere. It literally leads to the flat roof, with no egress. It is close to this location that I feel most "accompanied."

I have been told that the stairway to nowhere was created by a storm that caused severe damage to the third floor, which resulted in the removal of the top floor. Current tales relate that an elderly couple perished in the storm's damage to the third floor at some point in the building's history, which began sometime around 1900; however, I had little success verifying this assertion other than finding various mentions of the removal of an upstairs wall. In "Haunted House? Clancy Lowers the Boom," the August 19, 2008, edition of the *Louisville Eccentric Observer* states:

> The old Parisian Pantry at Bardstown Road and Bonnycastle Avenue was widely believed to be cursed by an angry ghost who remained inconsolable over the removal of an upstairs wall. A dozen short-lived eateries must have come and gone before Café 360 seemed to break the juju—perhaps they replaced the wall?[9]

Of the many eateries that served food at this address before Café 360 came along, the Parisian Pantry, which was operating during the 1980s, is a name that arises over and over. Many bloggers on Robin Garr's web-based restaurant guide, Louisvillehotbytes.com, including Garr herself, have told various renditions of the upstairs ghost-slash-removal-of-wall story. The tales sometimes mention the death of an old woman in an upstairs apartment, who haunted the upstairs yet became an angry spirit when the tenant after the Parisian Pantry removed an upstairs wall.[10] So the plethora of questions to this point includes the following: "Did anyone die, who were they and how—and when—was there a spirit or spirits that coexisted peacefully before becoming angry at some point, was the wall actually important or was there some other issue at hand, are spirits continuing to linger at 1582 Bardstown Road?"

Other than merely repeating the same ghost/wall removal/angry spirit story, I did uncover past tales of suspected haunted activity within the building. In 1985, during the Parisian Pantry's reign, a newly hired busboy found himself cleaning up a mess from coffee dripping down onto an empty warmer, where a coffee pot should have been waiting to catch it. The remainder of the staff not only denied preparing the coffee or removing the pot, they also refused to go anywhere near the beverage station, since the circumstances spooked them. At about the same time, a waitress was crying and trembling on the back steps and being consoled by other staff members. It seems that she had "seen and heard very weird things upstairs that messed with her." The crying waitress quit that very day. Years after that unsettling event, the former Parisian Pantry busboy would encounter former coworkers who would inquire if other similarly strange experiences were observed. Others had observed items out of place or being moved. In particular, salt and pepper shakers, organized one second, would be strewn about the next. Unexplained footsteps were also mentioned as common occurrences. The

Fig. 11: Stairs leading from first to second floor in Café 360. Although difficult to see, note the orb in the center of the 5th stair from the top.

young man's need to ask questions and recount his story ended with the phrase, "It is what it is."[11] Yes, it is what it is.

Over the past three years or more, I have talked with current staff and have heard Sanjay, Kasey, and Debbie relate many experiences, which include doors opening by themselves, flickering lights, cold spots, footsteps, objects that move about on their own, and perhaps even figures that may or may not present themselves. Listen to their experiences for yourself and make a determination. I have been through the building from cellar to upstairs and have felt accompanied even while "alone." I have been in rooms in total darkness. I have taken photographs (one has an orb, but no apparitions—those who know me well are privy to my stance on orbs: dusty old buildings that reveal orbs had better have the orb acting like a crazed UFO before I believe it is anything "supernatural"!). Some photos don't show detail when transferred from film to a book . . . the orb is in the center of the ninth stair from the bottom.

Among the many kinds of spirits that may or may not inhabit Café 360, the most important, in my opinion, are good people sharing good times!

Mark's Feed Store
Louisville

Mark's Feed Store has five Louisville-area restaurants, including the Highlands location at 1514 Bardstown Road. Their website, www.marksfeedstore.com, states their motto: "Friendly Folks Servin' Famous Bar-B-Q" with a commitment to deliver "WOW" service and "WOW" food to each and every guest. To this, I can only say—Wow . . . and I agree. The website boasts that the cooking style was handed down from a third-generation bar-b-q master from eastern Kentucky and that they use the finest pork, chicken, and beef slowly smoked over real hickory wood before being topped with their signature bar-b-q sauces. Their bar-b-q sandwiches are top notch, of course, but my personal favorite is the Salmon Burger, along with the best potato salad I've ever shoveled into my mouth, rounded off with a cold Corona.

Mark's Feed Store obviously is proud to continue another of Kentucky's favorite traditions—handing down recipes generation after generation so that Kentuckians can continue to greatly enjoy their food. Good food is certainly a prime part of a good life! And what's better than sharing one tradition while you're enjoying yet another tradition? Sharing a good ghost story, while eating traditional Bar-be-que, screams Kentucky just as loudly as horses and bourbon.[12]

The staff here is always as friendly as the website claims. I especially like to eat in the upstairs dining area overlooking Bardstown Road. It is here that I first felt a visitor near me while I ate by myself between an antique fireplace and an old closet that currently has no doors, since it holds only a table for storage. I feel a second presence in the basement, where there are only food pantries, coolers, and freezers. The upstairs woman's restroom has had many stories surrounding it. In fact, once during a tour of the building, I watched the water stop flowing with the knob turned in the "on" position. The water then fell from the faucet as if nothing had happened. There was no sputtering of water as there is when the water supply is shut off, and no knocking of pipes—just water refusing to flow and then once more allowed to flow. I have not been able to explain this event . . . except for ghostly activity.

Most of the staff here that I have worked with over the years have related tales of hearing voices, seeing things move or having been moved, and even glimpsing an apparition or two from the corner of an eye. Most recently, a plumber, alone in the building while working, reported a female voice saying "hello" and wishing him a good morning when there were no women present in the building. Sit down with Ann as she relates the repeated occurrence of an upstairs chair being removed from its stacked position on the table as floors are cleaned. This chair, on many occasions, has been found back on the floor, facing away from the table, with no employees having visited the area. Others have confirmed this; it has happened on more than one occasion with various witnesses. Many a nighttime closer has heard his or her name called while alone on the floor, or a lingering laugh, or footsteps where there are no persons to walk on the well-worn floors.

I have been told that an elderly man fell to his death down the side stairs when the building was a private residence and the stairs were used as a fire escape. Indeed, the house has quite a long history both as a residence and a number of restaurants. On the building's front, facing Bardstown Road, is an inscription dating the building to 1908. I have been unable to document any death occurring in the building, but I can certainly attest to a spectral presence. Over the past century, many a resident and visitor have shared stories of good food, loved ones who have passed, and the possibility of ghostly presences. Perhaps the stories of accidental death can be attributed to creative minds attempting to explain the unexplainable noises, voices, and moving objects. Or perhaps one or more persons did pass away over the many decades within the confines of this historic building. I feel that the ghostly activity persists due to a fondness for the structure, which is still decorated with a down-home country motif, as well as a fondness for the cooking of good food served to

39

family and friends that has saturated the very soul of the building. Mark's Feed Store has something for almost everyone—including spirits that enjoy the presence of fine folks enjoying fine food and sharing one of Kentucky's best traditions: the telling of a good story.

Odds and Ends

This chapter will have the longest conclusions section, which I refer to as Odds and Ends, due to the rapid changes that occur within the restaurant industry.

There are so many restaurants across the commonwealth, with stories or legends associated with them, that I apologize if I have excluded one of your favorites. Perhaps in another book?! Some of those that you may have heard of, or even visited, I myself have visited only to find them closed for business after so long in the food service industry. As stated, the restaurant business is one filled with change. The industry is demanding: long hours, tons of competition, hard work, dedication, and a passion for food excellence and customer service. Across the state, hundreds of restaurants open every year, and, sadly, many close before a reputation can be established. This transitory nature has had many victims as acclaimed restaurants—acclaimed both for their trademark foods and their ghostly reputations—have permanently closed their doors in recent years. The Phoenix Hill Tavern in Louisville, the Doe Run Inn and Restaurant in Brandenburg, and the Old Bethlehem Academy (turned restaurant) in Elizabethtown all had excellent reputations for serving good food in their respective genres, as well as ghostly legends associated with all. They are all, at the time of this writing, closed to the world of the living.

Others have changed their name and venue, such as the old Lock and Key Café in Georgetown. This former café had the distinct honor of a framed bullet hole in the wall that was the end destination of the suicidal bullet that killed a former bank president. His ghost was a frequent guest to the café.[13] This restaurant has since been closed and the space is currently a massage therapist studio aptly called the Studio. Tales continue regarding the Lock and Key Café, but the massage studio has occupied the space since 2012. By the signage placed outside, the current occupants appear proud of the building's ghostly past. And so they should!

With so many pieces of history lost, names changed, and persons forgotten along the pages of time, here I would like to make a plea—a plea for historical preservation. There are so many historic buildings listed on the National

Fig. 12: The Studio, Georgetown,
promising spooky times.

Register of Historic Places that are destroyed or permanently altered before they can be adequately protected or preserved. Others still never even make it onto the list and are unceremoniously destroyed. For years, I would routinely park near the Cherry Springs/Funk House and eat lunch in the parking lot while looking up at the 200-year-old windows. I could sense a ghostly presence from the parking area. It was just that strong. This was the old Dillon's Steakhouse on Hurstbourne Lane. After it closed, an upscale car lot opened, with its owner "tearing out 200-year-old plaster and woodwork and windows and covering historic brick with concrete veneer"[14] and making it look like a two-year-old prefab house. Plainly said, ignoring historical preservation destroys our historic places and our history.

So . . . that's one piece of history permanently altered beyond recognition. And another—John E's Restaurant, also in Louisville—is now gone forever. Although the historic cabin core of the restaurant was built in 1851 (or thereabouts) and was once the property of Revolutionary War hero George Hikes, and on the National Register of Historic Places (or was secretly removed from the list), the bulldozers struck before anyone could put a halt to the

Fig. 13: John E's Restaurant, Louisville. Behind the wrecking ball...enough to anger any spirit.

needless demolition. I happened to pass by on the day the haunted historic cabin was razed to the ground. The Hikes Family Cemetery remains nearby on the corner of Bardstown and Taylorsville Roads. Hall of Famer Louisville basketball coach Denny Crum was a spokesman for many years for this popular restaurant. The bar and lounge area offered a view of the neighboring cemetery—unique—creepy and cool all at the same time. Visiting the upstairs dining areas or the downstairs woman's restroom was an open invitation for a ghostly visit. Now, after the bulldozers have had their way, does the history and haunting still matter? Yes it does! History should be respected and preserved. Take a stand!

There! After I've stood up for the just and the true, after we've visited many of Kentucky's choicest restaurants, let's find a place to rest our heads for the evening—but just remember that the room you sleep in may have an unpaid guest sharing your space while you dream.

"The monster under my bed laughs
Yet I dare not laugh along."
—Yesenia Barkley

CHAPTER TWO

Haunted Inns and Hotels

Once upon a time, traveling meant finding temporary shelter along paths and then dirt roads. Travelers slept in their wagons, pitched a tent or lean-to, or slept under the stars next to a campfire. As civilization increased, roads became better and travelers stayed with relatives or friends until someone decided to give shelter to strangers and ask for compensation. Inns sprang up near stagecoach stops. This chapter has one of those. Inns grew into hotels and motels on the larger scale, while on a smaller scale houses with extra rooms became beds and breakfasts. The oldest inn we will explore in Kentucky is the Talbott Tavern in Bardstown . . . and what an inn it is!

Before our visits begin, or before you travel to these locations in person, remember who and where you are—a stranger in a strange place. The sounds you hear are unfamiliar to you. Sometimes it requires years to learn how a structure speaks in the wind or mumbles as foundations settle, to recognize the rattle of knocking pipes or the hum of a refrigerator motor, and the whoosh of a furnace blowing to life.

Inns and hotels have other guests coming and going, and people do some strange things that they consider normal. The outside traffic, both pedestrian and vehicular, is also unfamiliar. And the sights are new as well. Lighting, both natural and artificial, and the reflections off surfaces and the refractions through panes of glass can often play tricks on a mind that wants to see ghosts. Smells, touches, and "feelings" all can be altered by a mind that wants to believe.

That being said . . . let's go visit some haunted places!

The Talbott Tavern
Bardstown

Fig. 14: Talbott Tavern, Bardstown.

Bardstown, Kentucky, has a polished historical gem that serves Kentucky bourbon and tasty hot meals and has provided shelter to an impressive list of America's leaders and noteworthy persons since the late 1700s. Both the history and the ghostly activity of this impressive tavern and inn could literally fill not only chapters, but volumes. It will be painful, but I will keep this entry to a few pages!

During the latter half of the 1800s, Jesse James would hitch his horse outside, stroll into what is now the "oldest western stagecoach stop" still in operation, order whiskey, play cards, and then, on occasion, sleep off his gains or losses at the Talbott Tavern and Inn. In the darkened hours of slumber, he once awoke and let spray a volley of bullets at what he thought were birds or butterflies (depending on the source) as they disturbed his prized sleep time. Those bullet holes still exist in a faded mural in the Jesse James Room, which

Fig. 15: The 2ⁿᵈ floor landing at the Talbott Tavern. Historical items to make any of a number of spirits feel at home. Sit a spell and wait for good company to join you or just make an appearance.

has since suffered even more damage from a 1998 fire. At the end of the American Revolutionary War, frontiersman George Rogers Clark used the tavern and inn as a temporary base of operations. And there is still an unpaid bill that he failed to take care of. Other noteworthy historical figures who visited or slept at the inn include Daniel Boone, Andrew Jackson, William Henry Harrison, and the then-exiled Louis-Philippe of France. In fact, it was a member of the former French king's entourage who painted the mural that Jesse James would later shoot.[1]

When Abraham Lincoln was only seven years old, he stayed at the inn with his parents after a court ruling against the Lincolns ultimately led to their moving to Indiana. There is now a room at the inn that bears his name. Still more visitors include Henry Clay, John Fitch (inventor of the steamboat), George S. Patton, Washington Irving, Stephen Foster, and the wildlife artist and naturalist John James Audubon.

The old Talbott Tavern was built in 1779 on a parcel of land originally purchased by a man named Hynes; the tavern was called the Hynes Hotel or Hynes House. George Talbott purchased the tavern in 1886, and, within two years, six of his twelve children had perished there, including one who plummeted down the stairs, while another hanged herself after suffering an unrequited love.[2] [The stairs are visited by an orb shown in figure 16.] In fact, only five of his children survived to adulthood. The original tavern consisted of the current eastern rectangular structure, which is built of stone walls that are two feet thick and utilize heavy ceiling timbers. There were two separate fireplaces that were used for cooking as well as heat. The tavern originally had two guest rooms on the second floor, one for men and one for women—individual rooms for guests did not become widespread in the United States until the early nineteenth century. The brick western section was constructed approximately a century later.[3]

Fig. 16: Another staircase, another orb (second stair from top) also difficult to see. Talbott Tavern charm and the site of much ghostly activity.

Fig. 17: Many orbs in Pioneer Cemetery behind the Jailer's Inn right next door to the Talbott Inn.

That's a lot of history, and a lot of good folks—many would swear that more than a few of those who visited or lived in the Talbott Inn never truly left.

But why so many ghosts? Of course, there are the tragic deaths of the Talbott children. And, as author Jeffery Scott Holland succinctly states in his book *Weird Kentucky*, "It's almost a certainty that people died of illnesses and were murdered on the premises in the violent and chaotic frontier days of the eighteenth century."[4] Many people also died by hanging at the neighboring jail and gallows (see the entry on the Jailer's Inn), and there's even a cemetery just behind the Jailer's Inn. See figure 17 (with many orbs, of course). John Fitch, inventor of the steamboat, was interred in the cemetery in 1798, and his remains were removed and reburied under the memorial at Court Square in 1927. Over the years, many graves have been damaged by time and slow-moving plans (see figure 18).

And there are those who claim that Jesse James's dream was yet another apparition, and that his bullets passed through as easily as if it were a ghost. Other guests have had ghostly or precognitive dreams, such as Abraham Lincoln's dreaming of his own death. Look closely at the desecrated grave of Proctor

Ballard in Figure 18 and you will note that the sergeant was a member of George Rogers Clark's regiment during the Revolutionary War.

Indeed, the Talbott Tavern has had so many ghost sightings and haunting stories over the years that each of the guest rooms contains a continuing diary for guests to document their ghostly encounters for future visitors to enjoy. As shown in many of the previous photos, orbs appear in so many of my photos—always in the reportedly haunted places and

Fig. 18: Time-ravaged graves in the Pioneer Cemetery.

seldom in other locations. A friend who stayed with me in the Lincoln guest room had a nightmare of an angry man standing over her as she slept, and she is a self-proclaimed ghost skeptic who rarely has scary dreams. Personally, I certainly felt a presence in much of the Talbott Tavern but had no overt experiences or dreams—yet! I am soon due for another visit.

The extent of possible experiences may be summed up by the experiences of one overnight guest, as related in the previously mentioned book *Weird Kentucky*. During a single night when all rooms were vacant except for the room she shared with a friend, she experienced banging noises, moving shadows, doors slamming, water turning on and off, toilets flushing by themselves, cold spots, a man's sneeze outside her door, footsteps in the hallway, the chiming of a bell, horses' hooves, men talking and laughing, and finally the nightmare of a man hanging himself after she finally fell asleep after 5:00 a.m.[5]

After all of the previous descriptions of ghostly activity, the only thing remaining is a full-body apparition. It has been related that the heavy wooden timber from which the Talbott daughter hanged herself is still exposed in the tavern, and the "lady in white" apparition is a somewhat common vision throughout the inn and the bar. And there are plenty of haunts in the restaurant area as well.

Here is another entry where I will caution you, as reader and diner, of the possible physical manipulation of your surroundings as you dine. The following story from *Ghosthunting Kentucky* by Patti Starr demonstrates this fact perfectly. Patti herself was, at the time, manager of the inn and restaurant

Fig. 19: The Lincoln Suite in the Talbott Inn. He stayed here. Does he return to visit?

and responded to a complaint made by a diner. The diner asked if she could make his fork stop moving. Quite an interesting request when you think of it! When she approached the table where the diner was eating, she saw a fork balanced on the rim of his salad bowl, rocking back and forth. She reached down and pushed the fork down so that it rested on the bottom of the bowl. As she turned her gaze from the utensil to the diner, the fork once more slid up the side of the bowl without any assistance until it balanced once more on the rim of the bowl! Ms. Starr mentioned the presence of ghosts to the diner, and he and his family soon left.[6] Ghosts aren't for everyone. They are, however, for those of us interested in spirited dining! In fact, Bardstown, Kentucky, might very well be, street for street and house for house, the most haunted town in the US of A.

Let's travel next to the Jailer's Inn—right next door!

The Jailer's Inn
Bardstown

Inns or bed and breakfasts that have a long history of being frequented by ghostly visitors usually find avenues to cater to their nonghostly guests in ways that perpetuate the otherworldly tales that give identity to a locale. One frequently utilized method is a room journal, as mentioned in the Talbott Inn entry. Guests write down their experiences to share with visitors who follow. During my last visit to the Jailer's Inn in Bardstown, I shared, through written accounts, the stays from the previous fifteen months with guests from fourteen states in addition to Sweden and Australia. The descriptions used most often were that the waterbed was "super" comfortable, the breakfast was "extra" yummy, orbs were plentiful in photographs, and that the stay was extremely enjoyable even if most guests experienced unusual nightmares and were disturbed in their sleep . . . usually around 3:00 a.m. In fact, universally, after each entry where they relayed how poorly they slept, due to unexplainable voices, ticking noises, or the clacking of shackles . . . they immediately stated just how much fun their stay was.

Let me brief you on the details of the Jailer's Inn: the inn rests on land that was once known as the Old Nelson County Jail property and housed prisoners from 1797 until 1987. The current front building, referred to as the "Old Jail," was constructed primarily of limestone in 1819. It has thirty-inch-thick walls and once contained two cells and an "upstairs dungeon" that prisoners called home. The back building or "New Jail" was built in 1874 and is surrounded by a stone

Fig. 20: The Jailer's Inn, Bardstown.

Fig. 21: Actual jail cells within the Jailer's Inn.
Feels like home . . . for the guests of this life
and the next.

wall. Once the new structure was completed, the front building became the jailer's residence. This jail complex was at one time the oldest operating jail in the commonwealth of Kentucky and is listed on the National Register of Historic Places.[7]

Since the prisoners have gone, some say more than a couple have remained—curious guests can stay in one of the six beautifully decorated rooms located in the renovated front jail, or, if you prefer to experience the chilling and sobering conditions of the Old Nelson County Jail, try staying in the "jail cell" located in the rear. Step outside the rear door and into a courtyard where prisoners once crushed limestone or were hanged at the Nelson County gallows. Fun stuff! Well, it is if you like history and interesting and comfortable surroundings . . . and ghosts!

The most encountered spirit may be that of Martin Hill, who was convicted of murdering his wife in 1885. Mr. Hill shot her while she was at a neighbor's house, and was soon sentenced to hang from the gallows. However, before his execution date, he became extremely ill and passed on. It was reported that he spewed a shower of vile and obscene blasphemies during his fever-induced and painful delirium. Many prisoners and guests of the inn have claimed to hear Martin Hill's pain-filled cries and delirious rantings in the decades since his death. He is also accused of many of the other paranormal occurrences that take place throughout the building. His story was featured in a 1909 article about hauntings at the inn, which remains on display.[8]

According to the entries from the "jail cell's" journal, although many visitors experienced potentially ghostly phenomena, an equal amount did not—myself included. Ghosts are not performers that keep a schedule. Nor

Fig. 22: Courtyard at the rear of the Jailer's Inn. Hangings once took place here.

is every bump in the night a spectral occurrence. In fact, many comments made here at the inn are those that I regularly dismiss as easily explainable, such as the presence of orbs or noises or voices heard within a strange place while partially asleep. Such experiences are hardly supernatural. Most visitors who shared their experiences noted they had unusual dreams or nightmares during their stay. I attribute this as the sleeping mind merely acting on the many implants from the stories that preceded their slumber. I watched three hours of *The Walking Dead*, read scores of "haunted" experiences from the room's journal just before bed, came to the inn in high hopes of encountering a ghost . . . and not only did I sleep peacefully (and comfortably) without bad dreams, but I also did not hear a single unexplainable sound or voice. Yet—I am still a firm believer.

Some compelling experiences from visitors include the many malfunctioning electronic devices and the fact that most guests included 3:00 a.m. as the time when events happened. Some may have read the journal to plant such a thought, but far from all did. One visitor shared my impression: "most activity was in the courtyard!" Remember the gallows once dropped the condemned to their final reward right here in what is now the same place where visitors sip their morning coffee.

Fig. 23: The rear entry through the stone wall behind the Jailer's Inn. This is where prisoners were once brought to their new home. Some never left . . . alive.

My favorite remark came from a young boy who wrote: "I would not recommend staying here alone unless you like to be scared stiff. Great stay though!"

I did stay alone . . . and I love to be scared stiff! I will say overall—with or without a ghost in your room—the staff was very friendly, the rooms were clean and loaded with history, and the whole place was just plain fun. The journal reviews were spot on!

Historic Maple Hill Manor
Springfield

Midway between Bardstown and Perryville, along US Route 150, awaits the charming town of Springfield. While traveling through, there is no finer place to stay than Historic Maple Hill Manor. Built by slaves in 1851 for the Thomas McElroy family, this historic Greek Revival–style plantation house currently boasts a craft shop, an orchard, a nature preserve, and an alpaca and llama farm. The moody mammals are visible from Route 150 but come into clearer focus as you make your way up the long, winding drive. Once past the beautiful animals, step through the doors of the manor into another age—a quieter age where life was not always so fast, so stressful.

But times weren't always quiet or stress free. The Civil War battle at nearby Perryville, in the year 1862, was the largest engagement in Kentucky and took many lives. Many of the wounded were brought to the Maple Hill plantation for treatment. However, many died from their wounds. More than a few might claim that some of those Civil War soldiers never left the place of their

Fig. 24: Maple Hill Manor, Springfield.

death. Accounts of footsteps heard in empty rooms, cold spots on warm days, odd lights occurring in photographs, and prophetic or unusual dreams have been reported by many visitors.[9] Some have stated that the ghostly visits belong to former residents of the plantation, in addition to the soldiers. Notice the recurring theme of unusual or prophetic dreams within haunted locations—here, too, like those in the Talbott and Jailer's Inns in Bardstown.

The ghostly experiences are such a part of this manor that Maple Hill offers an annual ghost retreat held on weekends through the month of October. The two-night package includes a ghost trek, ghost stories and dessert, a presentation by a paranormal team, an actual ghost investigation, Tarot card and psychic readings, a cemetery tour, two breakfasts, and a pizza party. Got the shivers yet? I'm excited!

Springhill Winery Bed and Breakfast
Bloomfield

Just northeast of Bardstown waits another historic place to lay your head while listening for ghostly footsteps in the night. This beautiful plantation home offers a winery complete with wine-tasting events and a gift shop—in addition to the bed-and-breakfast accommodations. And if all of that weren't enough, there's plenty of history and, yes, ghost stories galore. Read a partial description from Springhill's website:

> Disclaimer: The history and stories that I'm about to recount are facts and folklore that have come from the *Kentucky Standard* newspaper, *Nelson County Encyclopedia*, and personal accounts of neighbors and family members who once lived in this home.
>
> The house is best known for three things: (1) the Civil War skirmish here in 1863; (2) the architecture of the home, such as the elaborate ironwork outside and woodwork inside; and (3) the many haunting ghost stories.
>
> This house was built in 1857–59 by John R. Jones, his wife and sons. Jones came here with a land grant for 1,050 acres and 40 slaves, 9 who attended the house and the others living in cabins along the perimeter of the land. One cabin is still partially standing in a grove of trees in a back field that you can see from the winery.[10]

The historic home is located at 3205 Springfield Road in Bloomfield. At the turn of the twentieth century, Dr. James Hughes traded his farm in Missouri to the remaining family of Mr. Jones. It was Dr. Hughes who imported the beautiful ironwork from Paris, France. He was also responsible for much of the remodeling of the plantation home.

However, along with beauty, life offers a darker side. And it is this darker side of life that perhaps explains many of the unexplainable happenings at the Springhill B&B. The original owner, John Jones, was murdered by Confederate guerillas in 1864, by the well in back of the house. Other skirmishes and deaths also occurred here during the years of the Civil War. There still exists an underground tunnel beneath the trap door to what was once the slave's quarters. One psychic reported that there were the remains of three dead infants born to slaves who never escaped along the "underground railroad" that brought slaves to their eventual freedom.[11] This tunnel has remained intact so as not to disturb the rest of the dead. Indeed, such dark moments might account for the many reports of doors opening and closing, chairs moving by themselves, and the sounds of children's voices. So, visit Bloomfield . . . have a glass of wine, wander the grounds, and listen for children in the house and underfoot. Sounds like a great night to me.

Gratz Park Inn
Lexington

Named for historic Gratz Park and early Lexington businessman Benjamin Gratz, the Gratz Park Inn is Lexington's only boutique hotel. Located at 120 W. 2nd Street, the tract of land where the inn now rests was first established in 1781. Twelve years later, it was purchased by Transylvania Seminary. The school's main building was destroyed by fire, and it subsequently moved across Third Street to its current location. Built in 1906, Gratz Park Inn's current structure first housed a medical clinic modeled after the famous Mayo Clinic. The Lexington Clinic moved in 1958, and the building was bought by an engineering firm before being turned into a luxury hotel in 1988. In 1958, Gratz Park became the first Designated Historic Area in Lexington.[12]

Since the luxury hotel opened in 1988, many guests and staff members have reported ghostly happenings. The sounds of a little girl running through the halls, laughing, and even playing jacks have disturbed many a guest. This

Fig. 25: Gratz Park Inn, Lexington.

little girl is heard but not seen and is known as "Lizzy." Staff members have witnessed the apparition of a black man in a plaid shirt whom they call "John," since journals found upstairs from the time when the building was Lexington's first clinic describe the patient and even record the very same words that he has uttered. The groundskeeper's office in the basement was once the clinic's morgue. History and mystery at this luxury hotel! Reports of lights turning on and off, and knocking on guest room doors when no one is on the other side, are not uncommon. Allegedly, an elderly gentleman who likes to startle housekeepers by turning on televisions has been spotted on the lower level. Contrary to most haunted-house legends, most ghostly sightings at Gratz Park Inn occur during daytime hours, though strange sounds have been reported all hours of the day and night.[13]

Reclining in a fine leather chair in the library just off the main lobby is a nice place to reflect on your thoughts and perhaps listen for Lizzy running through the halls with a playful laugh just around the corner . . . always heard . . . never seen. However, even if Lizzy and John choose to remain hidden, the Gratz Park Inn offers the best of Lexington and Kentucky hospitality.

Fig. 26: Leather and polished wood in the
lobby of the Gratz Park Inn.

Griffin Gate
Lexington

Located at 1800 Newtown Pike in Lexington, the Mansion at Griffin Gate Marriott Resort & Spa is a historic antebellum estate turned restaurant. The original structure was an Italian Villa–styled, two-story brick home with a three-story tower built in 1854 for David Coleman and family. This structure burned in December 1872. The current structure was designed by Cincinnatus Shryrock and completed in 1873; it was christened Highland Home. The Colemans continued to live in the new structure for a number of years. After the Colemans moved away, Mr. and Mrs. Charles Eveleth remodeled extensively and added the tall columns in the front to create the appearance of an antebellum mansion. The next owner, Alfred Marks, added antique mantels and paneling and changed the name to Griffin Gate.[14]

At about the same time that meals began to be served at special events in the historic structure, stories about hauntings began to accumulate. The structure is not open except at times of caterings and such, and a casual walk around the building brings with it a sense that you are not alone. Walk inside and the history will, at once, grab you. Something, or someone, else might as well.

David Coleman's daughter was named Greta. The stories relate that this teenaged girl hanged herself after being rejected romantically. And it is this sweet-sounding Greta who has been identified as the specter witnessed on the staircase, wearing a long gown, and has been further blamed for a long list of spectral occurrences, which include icy touches and tugs on dresses, the unscrewing of bulbs in the chandeliers, slamming doors, closing shutters, moving keys, locking guests in the upstairs bathroom, and an occasional girlish laugh. EVPs by various people

Fig. 27: The Mansion at Griffin Gate, Lexington, welcomes you.

have recorded her voice as well as what some claim to be her grandfather's.[15]

I have included the Griffin Gate in this chapter because it is a part of the Marriott Resort & Spa and is yet another example of the blurred lines that spirits cross, not just from the living to the dead to the living, but also across the multifunctionality of buildings and properties. Parks can have cemeteries, hotels have restaurants, and houses become restaurants and inns. The primary thing they all have in common is they house legends and stories of ghosts.

Fig. 28: The Mansion's doors wait to let
some in and to make sure some never leave.

The Campbell House
Lexington

The Campbell House in Lexington is located in the heart of the city near the University of Kentucky campus. Since its opening in 1951, it has evolved and adapted after bouts with fire in 1986 and extreme wind damage in 2009. Throughout it all, it has remained one of the premier hotels in the Fayette County area. The lobby is both unique and beautiful and the front entrance is as inviting as it is elegant.

Researching its haunted history finds the same story repeated over and over. Legends report the murder of two women on two separate evenings—a woman shot to death in a third-floor room, and a woman stabbed to death on a staircase, with blood stains persisting through time. However, since this hotel has had many renovations over the years, it is unlikely that blood stains have remained. I have not seen any recurring blood stains, nor did I encounter any slamming doors or any of the other "strange occurrences" reported on various haunted-location web pages. What I did experience was a beautiful hotel in a wonderful city. If you find anything of a different nature, please let me know.

I want to make a quick note here. The power of suggestion can be a powerful thing. Once someone hears that a murder has occurred somewhere, they automatically assume a ghost is present. Not so, of course. And the fact that I encountered the same couple of stories repeated almost word for word lends credence that people want to believe. I include entries such as this to respect those who have heard stories and investigated them. Some have even captured EVPs here. I cannot make the claim that just because I don't sense something on a particular visit that nothing ever occurs at such a site. You make the decision.

The Brown Hotel
Louisville

What do these things have in common? The Hot Brown sandwich is created. Hollywood legend Victor Mature works as an elevator operator. Al Jolson gets a shiner in a fistfight. A bell captain catches a fish in the second-floor lobby (during the 1937 Great Flood). Lily Pons, French American operatic soprano and actress, lets her pet lion cub roam free in her suite. World leaders

Fig. 29: The Brown Hotel, Louisville. So many
places for a ghost to appear and disappear.

and celebrities such as the Duke of Windsor, Harry S. Truman, Elizabeth Taylor, Robert Young, Joan Crawford, Muhammad Ali, Jimmy Carter, George H. Bush, and Barack Obama rest their famous heads.

There should have been enough clues for any Louisvillian to know the answer.

It all happened at the corner of Fourth Street and Broadway at the Brown Hotel, where Georgian Revival elegance greets guests with its timeless southern charm.

Oh, and there's a ghost, too. We'll get to that!

Built by prosperous Louisville businessman J. Graham Brown, the Brown Hotel began greeting guests on October 25, 1923, only ten months after construction began. The first person to sign the guest register was David Lloyd George, former prime minister of Great Britain. The sixteen-story concrete-and-steel hotel has 293 rooms and was built in the Georgian Revival style, faced in brick, and trimmed in stone and terra-cotta. The interior design is primarily of the English Renaissance style with Adams-period detail. It is listed on the National Register of Historic Places and holds the coveted AAA Four Diamond rating.[16]

Along Fourth Street in front of the hotel, there's a statue of Mr. Brown and his French poodle, Woozum. For many years, the pair lived in a small suite on the fifteenth floor. Brown died in 1969. Many guests and members of the staff have reported hearing footsteps and the sounds of furniture being moved on the fifteenth floor when no one is there. The elevator frequently stops at this floor for no reason. Well, Mr. Brown probably has a reason. The scent of his cigar is still detected (it's a nonsmoking facility). Some have even claimed to have seen footprints appear in the dust in infrequently traversed storage rooms.[17] One traveler added a tip on a travel guide website: "Ask for the one [room] with the ghost."

Fig. 30: Mr. Brown outside of his forever home.

I have stayed overnight here and greatly enjoyed the beautiful surroundings. I have also attended many conferences on the upper floors and felt a presence nearby as I sat in comfortable chairs and benches along the halls. I have lingered in empty and quiet rooms and have felt an overwhelming message that this is "home." Give it a try, and say hello to Woozum for me.

The Seelbach Hotel
Louisville

Just a couple of blocks north of the Brown Hotel is another of Kentucky's premier hotels: the Seelbach Hilto, Louisville. And just like the previous entry, this hotel is also filled with history, fascinating stories . . . and ghosts!

Even before it opened in 1905, its founders, Bavarian-born immigrant brothers Otto and Louis Seelbach, envisioned a hotel that would rival the best accommodations that Europe had to offer. This grand hotel has French Renaissance design and is listed on the National Register of Historic Places. It is an AAA Four Diamond Award–winning hotel as well. And the stories are among the best!

My favorite? Rock-and-roll legend Billy Joel, while staying at the hotel, once took time to relax by sitting at the piano at the bar and beginning to play. By the time he finished, fans were crowded out the door to catch a listen of this unrehearsed and free concert.[18] As much as I love ghosts and stories of ghosts, I admire such a man who loves his music and his fans enough to just be himself. Piano man, indeed!

The hotel's website fills us in on some of the other famous guests as well. George Remus, a Cincinnati mobster nicknamed the "King of the Bootleggers," earned a great deal of money by running whiskey northward during Prohibition. He would frequently spend time at the Seelbach, both for business and pleasure. Writer F. Scott Fitzgerald also visited the Seelbach during this period for its fine bourbon and cigars and was taken in by the charismatic Remus. In fact, the gangster became the inspiration for the title character in *The Great Gatsby*.

Famous gangster Al Capone also frequented the Seelbach, playing poker in what is now called the Oak Room. He presented a large mirror as a gift to the hotel and made it a practice always to face the mirror to keep an eye both on his competition and his back! Mr. Capone would place lookouts throughout the hotel, so that when the police came into the lobby, someone would step on a button, and the doors going into the poker room would automatically close, signaling his getaway.

His escape was through one of two secret passageways that have now been sealed. One passage went out and down to the street, while the other went downstairs to the tunnels beneath the hotel. He became an invisible man of sorts—traveling up to a mile away from the hotel without being seen.

Enter now . . . the ghosts. A staff member of the hotel's café reported seeing an elderly woman wearing ragged clothes standing next to a mirror and leaving no reflection. The employee turned to speak to the woman, but she faded from view as if she had never been there at all. A young couple on their honeymoon awoke to find a man standing by their eighth-floor window, looking out. They reported the room to be eerily cold. When they turned on the light, the man disappeared. Other guests have reported smelling the faint scent of perfume and hearing disembodied footsteps walk along the corridors.

The most famous apparition at the Seelbach, however, is the Lady in Blue. The woman ghost, most agree, is that of Patricia Wilson, who stayed at the hotel in 1936. Patricia was anxious to reunite with her estranged husband. They had agreed to meet at the Seelbach, but he never arrived. Shortly after she received the message that he had been killed in an accident, she took her own life. Her body, dressed in a long blue dress, was found at the bottom of an elevator shaft. Decades later, guests continue to see a beautiful but sad-looking brunette dressed in blue walking the halls, standing alone, or otherwise waiting still for her partner in life.[19]

History, grand accommodations, and more ghosts than you dare to count . . . what more could you ask for?

Christopher's Bed and Breakfast
Bellevue

Just how often do you get to sleep in church? I mean a sound sleep, and not just a short snooze until you start snoring? Perhaps that's what the owners were thinking when this old church, built in the late 1800s, was converted into a bed and breakfast. Located a mile south of downtown Cincinnati and an equal distance from the popular Newport on the Levee dining and entertainment complex, guests can experience something a bit unique. The name changed of course—it comes from the Catholic patron saint of travelers. What stayed the same were all the original stained glass and the hardwood floors. Since its opening in 1997, it has been voted best interior design, among other bests! Try it and see.

Perhaps a few ghostly visitors have also considered it to be the best, since they have remained. Since shortly after the renovations began in 1996, apparitions have been sighted on the stairs, unseen hands play the piano in the wee small hours, and disembodied voices and footsteps have also been reported by a number of guests.[20] Have you been to church lately? Maybe now you have a valid reason.

Odds and Ends

Like some of the restaurants in the previous chapter, many historical homes have been converted to other uses, and some have reverted back to private use as a single residence. Such is the case with Young's Inn—currently a private residence in West Point, Kentucky.

More than one travel site still lists this private residence as the Ditto House Inn. Not so! I visited in January 2016 to confirm its residential status. And for every travel site that lists the Ditto House Inn, there are a dozen websites that repeat the ghostly happenings that once occurred within this historic location.

This historic home, moving backward through time, has been a private residence, a bank, a ticket agency, a boarding house, a Civil War hospital and barracks for General William T. Sherman, and again a private residence. Young's Inn is on the National Register of Historic Places, and it is not uncommon to find coins, buttons, belt buckles, and other items from the Civil War troops who were once treated here. The building is constructed in the Federal style, primarily of brick, with exterior walls that are eighteen inches thick. The woodwork, staircase, banisters, and upstairs floors all are original. This inn is very close to the Ohio River, at the mouth of the Salt River just southwest of the suburban outskirts of the Louisville metro area.

Many visitors and guests over the years have claimed that at least a few of the soldiers who died after having been treated have stayed on as ghosts. Just as in some of the Civil War battlefields that we will visit in the next chapter, the combatants of the Civil War endured harsh lives and even more tragic deaths, such as those who were treated here at this temporary medical treatment center. A strong yearning to hold onto life or to say goodbye to loved ones often leads to spirit activity, and, over the years, people have reported apparitions attempting to communicate directly, face to face, and then disappearing right before their eyes. Others have even been physically touched. There is a nearby cemetery, as well as Ft. Duffield just across the highway, adding centuries of history to the vicinity. Ft. Duffield is a Union fortification constructed in the fall of 1861 to protect the Old L&N Turnpike. It is one of the largest and best-preserved earthwork forts in Kentucky.

Whether you stay at the inn or visit the historic Ft. Duffield, enjoy the local history that sometimes just doesn't know when to let go.

Just as in the previous chapter, there are so many other reportedly haunted places to stay that I could have written an entire book and still have left some out. Needless to say, in my opinion I selected most of the best (if I excluded a favorite—my apologies).

> "Ghosts could walk freely tonight, without fear of the disbelief of men; for this night was haunted, and it would be an insensitive man who did not know it."
> —John Steinbeck, *Tortilla Flat*

CHAPTER THREE

Haunted Parks and Natural Areas

Imagine this: It's late at night, a fog rolls in to obscure the moon, and the trees close in like menacing strangers rather than the friends they were in sunlight just a few hours ago. When you walk alone in such a scene it's easy to believe that the woods are haunted, especially when you throw in such factors as an unsolved murder or a missing child. Often, woods are also home to a long-abandoned house or a secluded graveyard. This chapter includes some of all of the above!

George Rogers Clark Park
Louisville

Before it was denied approval, George Rogers Clark Park in Jefferson County was the original site for the Louisville Zoo. However, even without that distinct honor, this urban park stands out as a place of historical—and ghostly—significance. The Clark Family Cemetery still rests within the boundaries of the park . . . even though General George Rogers Clark lies in eternal rest elsewhere. He was interred in Locust Grove (the site of his death, six miles upriver of Louisville and home of Clark's sister, Lucy Croghan) in 1818 and was exhumed in 1928, to be reinterred in Cave Hill Cemetery. The current lodge, built in 1951, still stands but a few yards from where the late general built a cabin for his parents in 1785, on a rise called "Mulberry Hill." The cabin was something of a landmark even in its own time due to the inclusion of glass windows—the first of any building in the city of Louisville. The other famous inhabitant of this park is a bald cypress tree that is currently behind a chain-link fence at the bottom of a hill adjacent to the playground and picnic area. There are two legends surrounding this very large, very old tree. The first: General Clark thrust his riding crop into the ground, and from that simple action grew this stately tree. The second is a legend that I grew up with in the 1960s and 1970s: a Native American brave was murdered and quickly and unceremoniously buried beneath the tree (or, as has been told, placed directly into a cavity of the cypress to be reclaimed by nature). When you visit the tree, look closely near the top of the tree's trunk for two, dark soulful "eyes" that are black as night and cast in deep shadow.

During research for an article on this tree, I discovered a letter to the *Louisville Courier-Journal* newspaper written in 1976, with the following line: "(P)eople in the neighborhood thought there was an old Indian buried under the tree." Yes, legends begin and legends grow, and such a letter corroborates the stories told to me as a child. The cypress tree has been verified by professionals to be old enough for General Rogers Clark to have planted it. It still stands tall and proud even though many other nearby trees have been felled by storms and tornados over the decades and centuries. In 1952, after the park had been denied as the site for the zoo and as the shelter house was being dedicated by various significant speakers, Mrs. Henry Bass, great-great-great-niece of General Clark, commented, "cursed be he that removeth his neighbor's landmarks." Drama and emotions have obviously run high and proud on occasion! As you visit the family cemetery, count the headstones—there are seven lined in a row. The final marker records the tragic loss of six-year-old Robert and ten-month-old Henry Stanard.

Tragedy, death, curses—but ghosts?

Indeed, history abounds and mystery awaits.

Imagine . . . the frontier wilderness in the late 1700s on a cold autumn night with a slight dusting of snow beneath the surreal light of a full moon. Add some people, real people, say, General George Rogers Clark and some others . . . and a Native American brave crouching beside a cypress tree on a hill called "Mulberry." Who's to say what happened next.[1]

Jenny Wiley State Resort Park
Prestonsburg

Our easternmost destination in this chapter is Jenny Wiley State Resort Park, near Prestonsburg in Floyd County, Kentucky. This beautiful park is nestled upon the Appalachian Plateau and is bordered by Dewey Lake. Among the features available to guests: the forty-nine-room May Lodge with its 224-seat restaurant called the Music Highway Grill, an amphitheater with live entertainment, eighteen cottages, a 121-site campground, boating at the lake, and hiking along the many trails. And ghosts.

The park is named for a young pioneer woman—Jenny Wiley, of course—who was captured in 1789 by a group of eleven Native Americans: Cherokee, Shawnee, Wyandot, and Delaware among them. Three of her children and her younger brother were killed before her eyes. She and her fifteen-month-old son were taken alive, but her son was soon killed as well since carrying the child slowed her as well as her captors down. She delivered a baby boy who was killed at three months of age. Jenny was allowed to live and she performed chores until she escaped. After swimming across the Big Sandy River, she was finally reunited with her husband, Thomas, in the fall of 1790. They had five more children together, and she lived until the age of 71, passing away in 1831. Her grave is north of Paintsville in River, Kentucky, where she spent her final years. Wow—what a story![2]

In addition to the deaths at the hands of tribesmen and settlers, there have been a number of accidental drownings in Dewey Lake over the years, deaths by natural causes at the large lodge, and even a murder-suicide on one of the many trails. There are also cemeteries on the grounds. With a history such as this, it would be unusual for ghosts NOT to haunt this area!

The lodge tends to harbor most of the ghostly incidents … shadow figures have been witnessed, many have reported the apparition of a man entering empty rooms or hanging around the lobby, and cold touches from invisible hands have been felt; in addition, ghostly pushes, items knocked to the floor from tables, belongings moved from one place to another, the clatter of dishes or pots and pans, and other assorted noises emanating from an "empty" kitchen have been described.

In attempts to document such a large number of ghostly incidents, there have been a number of paranormal investigations that have occurred at the lodge, including visits by acclaimed Kentucky resident Patti Starr. She relates some very credible EVP responses in her 2010 book *Ghosthunting Kentucky*.[3] You can explore for yourself.

Personally, I believe that Jenny found her peace by mothering five children and sharing their lives. Her horrific tale had been put behind her. Others, however, may find such a beautiful place difficult to leave.

Jenny Wiley Gravesite
River

The town of Paintsville (population 3,459 according to the 2010 census) lies approximately midway between Jenny Wiley State Park and the frontier woman's final resting place. From Paintsville, take Euclid Avenue (Highway 40) east to Highway 581 and follow the narrow, serpentine, two-lane road to the volunteer fire department house on the left. This seven-mile journey along Highway 581 takes you through clusters of small-town houses, across railroad tracks, and among loads of impatient drivers. Perhaps I caught them on a bad day! Take your time. And if you are caught by a train, expect to wait a few minutes!

The firehouse is in the town of River, Kentucky, and it sits beside the local community center. Its parking lot has ample space for you to catch your breath from the drive on the two-lane narrow road. There's a path on the left of the parking area that leads you across a little stream and past a small cemetery before delivering you to Jenny Wiley's grave and monument. Her husband, Thomas Wiley, also has a monument that faces hers, but he was laid to rest elsewhere . . . in a small cemetery on an even-smaller hill near the mouth of Tom's Creek before the land was farmed, plowed under, and forgotten.[4]

In fact, the grave marker here at the cemetery in River, Kentucky, currently protected by metal bars, was once all that told the ages where this brave pioneer woman was laid to rest. Look closely at figure 31—there are no dates, no names . . . just a stone. That changed in 1965, when the monument was dedicated (figure 32). Jenny, her husband (Thomas), and their five children lived near this marker on their farm near Tom's Creek for

Fig. 31: "Iron bars do not a prison make." The original (?) grave marker of Jenny Wiley.

Fig. 32: Monument to Jenny Wiley, dedicated November 27, 1965.

decades with the horrible memories of murder, kidnapping, and infanticide. Now, under a canopy of trees, as clouds roll by and the cicadas screech and owls hoot, there is a solemn place here.

I would like to think that Jenny lived through her horrors and has no need to haunt this cemetery or any other place. Lie on the ground next to her grave and touch the sky with your mind and your heart . . . reach for a dream here in the wooded cemetery and see if you can't share a sliver of Jenny's peace.

Wickliffe Mounds State Historic Site
Wickliffe

Travel as far west in the commonwealth of Kentucky as the roads will allow, and you will find the town of Wickliffe and, within the town, the Wickliffe Mounds State Historic Site, located at 94 Green Street. This is a site of significant historical and archaeological value. The Kentucky State Parks website describes the area as follows:

A Native American village once occupied the site of Wickliffe Mounds, about A.D. 1100 to 1350. Here, people of the Mississippian culture built earthen mounds and permanent houses around a central plaza overlooking the Mississippi

River. Today, this Native American Indian archaeological site features mounds surrounded by abundant wildlife, museum exhibits, a walking trail, welcome center, a gift shop and picnic areas.

Open to the public since 1932, the museum exhibits the excavated features of two mounds with displays of Mississippian pottery, stone tools, artifacts showcasing their way of life and artwork, the archaeological history of the site, and the architecture of mounds and houses. Visitors have a spectacular view of the bluff area on top of the Ceremonial Mound, the largest mound on the site. Special exhibits, hands-on displays, demonstrations, and educational programs occur at various times throughout the year.

Scientific archaeological research through Murray State University has revealed important information about the Mississippian people here. This registered archaeological site is on the National Register of Historic Places, and a Kentucky Archaeological Landmark.[5]

The reason that this site is included in a book of ghost stories is the haunting mystery that remains with us. The native peoples here buried over 450 of their dead in Mound "C," where they stayed for nearly 600 years before they were exhumed and put on public display. In 2012, a ceremony took place as the remains were reburied at Wickliffe. With so many bodies desecrated, such a place is ripe for a potential haunting, but what is even more mysterious than the presence or absence of ghosts is the total lack of comprehension as to why these people vanished. Without signs of war, or famine, or disease . . . the settlement and all its peoples, a way of life that had sustained itself for two and a half centuries, fell apart for no discernible reason, and the tribes simply and completely vanished from Wickliffe.[6] Such happenings should haunt all thinking souls. Figure 33 is a photo of Ceremonial Mound "A," where religious, economic, and political activities took place. This was the tallest and largest mound and thus was closer to the heavens for the sake of ceremonies.

Plenty of history waits here at Wickliffe Mounds, and more than a hint of mystery as well. Now let's head west and then south, where the river meets the sky.

Fig. 33: Ceremonial Mound "A" at Wickliffe
Mounds State Historic Site.

Cumberland Falls
State Resort Park
Corbin

This is one of the most beautiful parks in the state of Kentucky, if not the world! The ghostly legend here is just another bonus. This natural area, aside from the falls, which comes complete with a regularly scheduled moonbow (yes—you read that right, an arc of misty light visible only during a full moon at the falls), also includes challenging hiking trails with beautiful rock formations, plentiful wildlife including deer and black bears, horseback riding, camping, a lodge with business accommodations and a restaurant, and semisecluded cabins. The falls are sixty-five feet high and 120 feet wide, but during flood stage they can swell to 300 feet wide. So much beauty is present that it has been nicknamed the "Niagara of the South."

Figure 34 shows the falls from "Lover's Leap." It is evident from the photo that the force of the turbulent water at the base of the falls would present a formidable challenge even to the best of swimmers, should a person accidentally fall in (NO wading or swimming is allowed). The apparition is frequently seen rising from the mist at the base of the falls among the rocks and water.

The ghostly legend here at Cumberland Falls follows a common theme where there are natural dangers nearby. I will include the legend below as related by kentuckyghosts.com. Most of the description is included here, but the website will supply additional information as well as other ghostly legends.

"The Ghost Bride of Cumberland Falls has been appearing in the park since the 1950s. The legend says that a young couple who had been married one afternoon came to spend their honeymoon in one of the cabins near the falls. In the early evening, the tired but exited couple went for a walk, still wearing the clothes they had been wearing at the ceremony. The man took his camera along with him, ready to take photos of the natural beauty of the falls and the glowing beauty of his new bride.

Fig. 34: Cumberland Falls State Resort Park. What a view!

Fig. 35: Cumberland Falls: stairs at night.
These are along the path leading to the falls.

The young woman decided she wanted a picture of herself in her wedding dress with the falls in the background. Climbing up a nearby hill in the cool evening light, the woman playfully danced near the edge of the cliff, filled with joy at beginning her new life. But that life came to a sudden, unexpected end. Moving towards the edge of the cliff to pose, the young bride lost her footing and slipped off the cliff edge, hitting her head on a rock and drowning in the swiftly-moving waters beneath the falls.

The unfortunate young girl still seems to be waiting for the excitement of her wedding night. Ever since her death, people have reported seeing the ghostly figure of a woman in a white wedding dress near the falls.

The most common sightings of the Ghost Bride happen at the top of the cliff near where he fell. A road now goes along that cliff, with a sharp curve right near the fatal overlook. Many park visitors have reported seeing the figure of a woman in a wedding dress run in front of their car as they come around this curve. If anyone stops, the bride inevitably disappears without a trace.

The second, and more spectacular, manifestation of the Ghost Bride of Cumberland Falls happens on the night of the moonbow. A moonbow is a phenomenon produced by moonlight refracting off of water in the air, in the same way that sunlight produces a rainbow. Cumberland Falls is the only place in North America where a moonbow can predictably be seen. Tourists commonly gather on nights of the full moon to see this beautiful effect of the soft light. But sometimes, people gathered to see the moonbow will see more than they were expecting. It's said that some nights, when the moonbow is at its peak, at the base of the cliff where the young woman fell, a ghostly figure dressed in a white wedding gown can be seen rising up out of the waters.

The famous story of the Ghost Bride of Cumberland Falls attracts many visitors and curiosity seekers to the park. The story has left its impression on the park, so much that the cliff where the bride fell to her death is now known as Lover's

Leap. If you go in search of an encounter with the phantom bride, even if you don't see her, you may well fall in love with the scenic beauty of one of Kentucky's natural wonders.[7]

The beautiful DuPont Lodge, as well as the falls, is reported to have ghostly visitations from the new bride. The photo on the right is of the great room just behind the reception desk.

Fig. 36: The great room at the DuPont Lodge at Cumberland Falls.

Whether you stay at the lodge or camp, view the moonbow, catch a glimpse of the ghost, or just stare at the waterfall, Cumberland Falls is a must-see for any visitor to our beautiful commonwealth.

Young Park
Harrodsburg

This is one of the best ghost legends ever . . . anytime . . . anyplace. Imagine dancing the night away until falling over dead in the arms of your partner! Whether you attempt to grasp the viewpoint of the one dying or the person left holding the once-vibrant dancer—this is a traumatic event. Events such as this define what we view as reasons to haunt this world from the afterlife. Young Park, on Linden Avenue in Harrodsburg, Kentucky, is little more than a picnic area and a playground with some open space to fly a Frisbee or toss a football on a summer's afternoon, but right up front at the tip of your car's bumper is a white picket fence surrounding a single grave.

However, during the mid-1800s, this area was the place to be. The Harrodsburg Springs Hotel once stood at this site, with the healing waters of nearby Graham Springs promising the well-to-do prosperous times and good health. There was ballroom dancing and live music, good food, and flowing bourbon. Regardless, they were not *all* good times. At one of these social events, a young woman danced herself to death, and many claim her ghost still walks the grounds.

Although many know the legend of the events on the night of this woman's death, her identity has remained a mystery. The woman had apparently registered at the hotel under a false name. She danced with several partners in the hotel ballroom, and all the men lined up for a chance to dance with her. At the end of the night, and without warning, she simply died in her last partner's arms. The staff and guests held a funeral for her and, not knowing her identity, quickly buried her on the hotel grounds. The hotel burned down decades ago, but her grave still remains, under a marker that reads: "UNKNOWN—Hallowed and Hushed be the place of the dead. Step Softly. Bow Head." Local lore says her ghostly form still appears, dancing in the moonlight.

I heard this account from many and read the nearly identical account in books and on websites as if all had read the same story going back 150 years or more.

There was one story, however, that stood out because it had quite a bit more information. In the September 5, 2002, edition of *Mercer's Magazine*, a headline boasted that the mystery had been solved. "Old Mystery Is Cleared Up. Identity of Woman Who Danced Self to Death Finally Established—or Is It?" The article had this to say about the mysterious dancer:

When [he was] a boy about 10 years old, living at Tazewell, Tenn., Joe Sewell, who was 40 years old then, told me about his wife "dancing herself to death at Harrodsburg." Her maiden name was Molly Black, and she was Sewell's second wife. I think they were estranged at the time, as Sewell had a spirit of wanderlust and at the time of her death he was on the road with a show.[8]

A second part of that same article was from an investigator from Tennessee who had attempted to verify such claims. He was able to verify the existence of Joe Sewell

Fig. 37: Young Park grave of the unknown dancer in Harrodsburg.

Fig. 38: Remnants of the old spring at Young Park.

from Tennessee but could not document his second wife, Molly Black, as being the woman who died and currently haunts the park in Harrodsburg, Kentucky.

As I strolled through this clean park on a warm afternoon, I of course saw no ghostly woman dancing in the moonlight. I did feel a certain pull toward the remnants of an old well near the grave (see figure 38). Night or day, stroll through this parcel of land and hum along to the tune of the '70s rock band King Harvest as they sing "Dancing in the Moonlight." If it is nighttime and a lone woman comes dancing along . . . kick your heels up and enjoy!

Old Fort Harrod State Park
Harrodsburg

As mentioned earlier, one of my favorite parts of ghostly activity is the history involved. This entry entails a rich lesson in history involving reports of a headless ghost at Fort Harrod in Harrodsburg, as reported by Alan Brown in his book *Haunted Kentucky*. After the Battle of Point Pleasant (West Virginia) in 1774, Captain James Harrod and others[9] returned to Harrod's Town. This battle was the first confrontation of the Revolutionary War. Although this claim to be the first battle of the war is refuted by many, it nonetheless left many of Virginia's militia, as well as members of the Shawnee and Mingo tribes, dead or mortally wounded.[10]

Upon their return, Harrod and his men found that the large natural spring that supplied water to the fort had washed away part of the garrison built the previous year. Construction soon began on a second, and larger, fort on what we now refer to as Old Fort Hill. This new fort was built on higher ground and, therefore, improved the view to watch for approaching enemies such as the hostile tribes that fought in the Battle of Point Pleasant.

Life was good for the settlers at Fort Harrod, with plentiful food such as bear (which substituted for bacon) and other game animals. The farming here was also good and included the "three sisters" of early American agriculture—squash, corn, and beans. Ideal pastureland surrounded the fort, where cattle grazed on grasses nourished by the limestone-rich soil. Several nearby springs provided water to the settlers, but the spring inside the fort supplied most of the needs of the community. Fort Harrod's most famous ghost story revolves around this spring.

The Old Fort Spring was located at the bottom of a hill in the fort's northwest corner and became a repository for the wastes both from people and animals after a stockade was built near the spring's location. An elderly Dutchman, Barney Stagner, was responsible for preventing carcasses of dead animals from being dumped into the spring and thus polluting the fort's primary water supply. One morning in June, some of the fort's inhabitants found Barney's horse grazing near the stockade—but Barney was missing. Missing, that is, until they discovered his decapitated corpse lying near the spring in the northwestern corner of the fort. His head was found on the sharpened point of a lance stabbed into the ground.

These images are so vivid (and perhaps exaggerated) that a variation of the legend involves Barney drinking with friends and then being attacked by members of a hostile tribe as he staggered home alone. Either way—poor Barney lost his head . . . literally.

The current Old Fort Harrod State Park is located across the street from where the original fort once stood. The spring where Barney was viciously murdered is behind the high school by the Lions Club building, where schoolchildren have reportedly witnessed the headless apparition of Barney Stagner. Some have seen the ghost's outstretched hands grasping out as if in a desperate search for his missing head.[11]

Fig. 39: Replicas of Revolutionary War-era cabins at Old
Fort Harrod State Park. Ghostly things happen here.

Within the perimeter of the current Old Fort Harrod State Park there are reports of ghosts as well. Replicas of cabins such as those where Harrod and his men once lived were built next to the original cemetery, where the original fort's inhabitants were interred from 1775 until 1833. (I have included photos of the replicated cabins above as well as the historical cemetery on page 83.) Captain James Harrod ironically is not buried within this cemetery; his body lies in an unmarked and unknown grave somewhere, since he mysteriously never returned from a hunting expedition.

Cabin number 9 has had a number of unexplained happenings, including sightings of an apparition at the top of the stairs. People hear otherworldly voices in the conference center, including the command to "get out." One woman reported being pulled to the ground by her hair! And apparently lights go on and off by themselves, mysterious noises are heard, and many people feel "eerie" just being there.[12]

After discussing so much of the "supernatural," we cannot leave this state park without mentioning one magnificent example of the "natural"! The osage

Fig. 40: Unmarked graves at Old Fort Harrod Cemetery.

orange tree pictured on page 84 has been standing since the late eighteenth century. It is over eighty-eight feet tall with a crown of seventy-six feet. The tree is taller and broader than the national champion of its kind, but it remains "unofficial" due to its split trunk.Standing in the presence of this wonder of nature or posing on one of its limbs that run parallel to the ground makes the trip to Harrodsburg more than worthwhile even if no ghosts are seen! Visit this park and explore a good portion of Kentucky's history—the cabin where Abraham Lincoln's parents (Thomas and Nancy Hanks Lincoln) were married has been transferred from Washington County to stand within the park, and George Rogers Clark conceived many of his plans right here within the fort. Even without the mystery, the history is astounding! Harrodsburg holds a gem… with the spirits loving it as much as I.

Fig. 41: The beautiful Osage-orange tree on the
grounds of Old Fort Harrod State Park.

Perryville Battlefield State Historic Site
Boyle County

Parks and natural areas not only offer great beauty but also preserve tremendous amounts of our nation's history. And there are no other preserved spaces where you would expect to encounter ghosts more than sites where deadly battles took place. Perryville Battlefield State Historic Site, near Perryville, Kentucky, in Boyle County, offers scenic vistas that look much the same today as they did when one of the bloodiest battles of America's Civil War took place on October 8, 1862. There is also an interpretive museum located near where many Confederate soldiers killed in the Battle of Perryville were buried. At 745 acres, it is the largest preserved Civil War battlefield in the commonwealth of Kentucky. Many monuments, informative signage, and cannons throughout the park detail notable events that occurred during the pivotal battle. This site became a part of the Kentucky State Park System in 1936.[13]

Every October there is a reenactment of the great battle where players choose sides and play out the scene where nearly 7,600 young soldiers were killed, wounded, or went missing over 150 years ago. However, many visitors and actors of this great reenactment claim that not all of those souls who gave their lives are missing. Many people report seeing and hearing the ghosts as they remain here at the site of their death. The battle that took place on central Kentucky's fertile soil was the South's final serious attempt to gain possession of the state that served as a border between the North and the South. In fact, Kentucky ranks highest of all the states where brother fought brother or father fought sons, since Kentuckians fought for both sides.

Perhaps it is for such reasons that so many spirits remain restless. Lee Kirkland, founder of the Spirit Hunters of Central Kentucky, reported in June 2015 that ". . . full-bodied apparitions [have been] seen still marching, several have heard the deep percussion of heavy artillery and cannon fire echoing across the rolling hills, and disembodied voices [have been] caught on digital recorders that give intelligent responses to questions that were indicative to 1862."[14] And some very compelling evidence has been recorded by the Travel Channel's *Ghost Adventures* team of Zak Bagans, Nick Groff, and Aaron Goodwin, who have visited the battlefield twice. In 2011, they visited Rocky Point Manor (season 5, episode 8). Three years later they revisited the battlefield and nearby areas while focusing on an additional two commandeered family homes that suddenly became field hospitals—the H. P. Bottom House and the Dye House (season 8, episode 11). Bullet holes still perforate the Bottom House, and so much blood was lost during the emergency operations both at the Bottom and Dye Houses that the stains remain to this day. Doors were removed from their hinges to serve as operating tables where soldiers died or had limbs amputated . . . blood spilling into the cracks in the floors and bodies being buried in mass graves nearby.[15]

The history at Perryville Battlefield State Historic Site includes death and misery—and ghosts . . . if you believe the hundreds upon hundreds of stories and sightings.

Natural Bridge State Resort Park
Slade

It is simply amazing just how much natural beauty exists within the state of Kentucky! Along the Middle Fork of the Red River, adjacent to the Red River Gorge Geologic Area and surrounded by the Daniel Boone National Forest in the counties of Powell and Wolfe, is the Natural Bridge State Resort Park. The natural wonder and star attraction here is a sandstone arch seventy-eight feet long and twenty feet wide. It is not huge by any means—at a thickness of just over twelve feet it rises sixty-five feet above the forest floor—but it offers an astounding view of the surrounding forest as well as other sandstone rock formations formed by at least a million years of weathering.

As early as 1889, the Kentucky Union Railway was bringing visitors in to marvel at the natural splendor as the railroad company sought to utilize the

Fig. 42: The "underside" of Natural Bridge State Resort Park in Slade, Kentucky.

area's timber resources. For decades, the only way into the depths of this forest was by foot or by train, and by the early 1900s the Lexington and Eastern Railroad was transporting as many as 25,000 visitors a year, mostly from the cities of Louisville and Lexington. The state took ownership of 2,400 acres in 1926 as a gift from the Louisville and Nashville Railroad. The park's acreage includes a four-acre pond, with the one-acre Hoedown Island at its center. There are eighteen miles of hiking trails (built by the railroad) within the park amid camping sites and a large portion (1,188 acres) that has been set aside as a nature preserve. The last trains came into the territory in 1942, after the local roads had made the area accessible by automobile.[16] An old train tunnel still exists under the Hemlock Lodge, although it has been fenced off to prevent injuries from falling rocks.

Enter . . . the Purple Lady! Over the years, many witnesses have claimed to see the ghost of a woman wearing a long purple gown in several parts of the park—including the Hemlock Lodge, Hoedown Island (where she left footprints in the snow), and areas within the Whittleton Campground. Many have guessed that she arrived by train during those early days of visitation and still waits for

Fig. 43: Sandstone and trees for miles and miles at Natural Bridge State Resort Park.

Fig. 44: A lizard friend. Along with the ghosts, one of the other inhabitants at Natural Bridge.

someone who never arrived, since she is spotted wearing her purple gown, often carrying her shoes, and sporting hair wound tightly in a bun as she lingers in the lobby of the Hemlock Lodge above the old train tunnel.

Another common story involved the alleged murder of a young woman in a cabin within the area that later became the Whittleton Campground. The old cabin burned down long before the campground was established. Perhaps she wanders the trails looking for her killer or maybe just hoping to find refuge in the missing cabin. Others claim that she may be the unfortunate victim of an accident, since hikers occasionally fall from ledges and arches to meet their demise. Perhaps the purple gown is but a pleasant memory from before the horrific accident. Regardless of who she is, many have seen her standing by the campground entrance or smiling in the lodge lobby before disappearing before their eyes!

I saw many natural wonders while at Natural Bridge, and several tiny souls such as the lizard in figure 44 that basked in the sun while searching for insects to eat. Perhaps there are spirits such as the Purple Lady searching for sustenance of another kind. Look for her while you're there, and definitely watch your step while on the arch. That first step is a killer!

Mammoth Cave National Park
Mammoth Cave

Some places have such a history, of ghosts and otherwise, that entire volumes could be written . . . and have been! It is for this reason that I am mentioning Mammoth Cave National Park only briefly. This is the world's longest known cave system and has had more than 400 miles of its passages explored. An early cave guide, Stephen Bishop, described the cave as a "grand, gloomy, and peculiar place,"[17] but it is named for its sheer size. Its status as a national park was established in 1941, and it is truly a natural wonder of worldwide significance.

On the ghostly side, it has been called "the most haunted natural wonder in the world." Park rangers, who often serve as tour guides, call the aforementioned Stephen Bishop the most frequently sighted apparition. He is buried in the Old Guide Cemetery, not far from the cave, and is often seen during the Violet City Lantern Tour. As if the caverns weren't dark enough, this tour is lit only with kerosene lamps. Outside the cave, near one of the park's remaining "consumptive" cabins, is a slab of stone where the bodies of dead patients were placed before burial after having succumbed to tuberculosis. For a brief period during the 1800s, a number of cabins were built to house patients. Today, that slab of stone is known as Corpse Rock, and many visitors have claimed to have heard phantom coughing originating here.[18]

Explanations for the cave's hauntings include the following: the many accidental deaths from the years the caves were mined for saltpeter, Native Americans who became lost in the cave, stranded travelers, missing cave explorers, the tragic tuberculosis victims, and perhaps even those who fell in love with the beauty of the site and simply chose not to leave.

An apparition that is occasionally seen, and heard, on the underground Echo Lake might be that of a young woman named Melissa. The February 1858 edition of *Knickerbocker Magazine* ran a story titled "A Tragedy in Mammoth Cave" that tells of young Melissa playing a cruel trick on her tutor after he refused to return her affections. Mr. Beverleigh, Melissa's tutor, was from Boston and began courting a neighbor girl, which set in motion Melissa's plans of revenge.

She had grown up in the vicinity of the cave and had traveled it often. She lured the young man inside the cave and abandoned him on the silent and dark waters of Echo Lake. He was never seen again. She later contracted tuberculosis and, having never released the guilt of her actions with Mr.

Beverleigh, emptied her soul before she died. Since her guilt led her to find the missing young man, she had returned to the cave day after day, exploring underground, calling out to him—all to no avail.[19] Thus, in the decades since, many have heard her calling out or coughing in fits. Which is the more extreme tragedy? Her painful death, coughing up blood and gasping for air? Her years of guilt? Her refusal to move on from the site of her accidental killing of an innocent man? Haunting questions one and all!

Floyd Collins is probably the most famous resident spirit of the Mammoth Cave system. Mr. Collins was an avid cave explorer as well as an accomplished businessman who was always looking for new caves that could be developed and made into a moneymaking enterprise. The term "Cave Wars" is often used for this period of history in central Kentucky. Floyd Collins was the former owner of Crystal Cave—a cave once believed to be a completely separate cave and once operated as a private attraction. Crystal Cave is located along Flint Ridge and is now well within the boundaries of Mammoth Cave National Park. Mr. Collins was trapped in the cave and died after an extensive rescue effort was conducted. Many apparitions throughout the entire cave system are attributed to Mr. Collins. There are a number of excellent books on these subjects, and, indeed, any time spent researching Floyd Collins and the "Cave Wars" of Kentucky would be time well spent. Equally, time spent in the majesty of Mammoth Cave, whether or not ghosts are seen or heard, will be among some of the most memorable moments of any life.

Odds and Ends

Haunted or not, Kentucky has a number of excellent Civil War battlefields in all parts of the state. Visit one in your area or while traveling; they include Camp Wildcat in London, Middle Creek in Prestonsburg, Mill Springs in Nancy, and Tebbs Bend in Campbellsville. Enjoy the history, and remember, just because there are no ghost stories circulating (or perhaps I have missed a few) doesn't mean they are not haunted. With so many lives cut short and so much pain and grief present at one time, every battlefield would be a likely place for a haunting.

However, for those of you who crave reports of haunted battlefields, try Blue Licks Battlefield State Park in Mount Olivet (Robertson County). This area has a long and interesting history. The Lower Blue Licks were a mineral spring and salt lick that attracted large herds of bison long before settlers found their way here. In 1782, one of the last battles of the American Revolution was decided at this location; the patriot troops included Daniel Boone and John Todd (ancestor of Mary Todd Lincoln). The springs were popular in the nineteenth century before they ran dry by 1896. As for reports of hauntings over the years . . . spirit voices and apparitions of Native Americans, soldiers, and early settlers are still seen and heard along the trails. Some have reported the ghostly voice of a "friendly" woman at the lodge.

We've traveled many roads and highways to reach all these parks and natural areas. Next, we'll travel some of those same roads and highways, only in the company of ghosts and agitated spirits.

"I shall be telling this with a sigh
Somewhere ages and ages hence:
Two roads diverged in a wood, and I—
I took the one less traveled by,
And that has made all the difference."
—Robert Frost, "The Road Not Taken"

CHAPTER FOUR

Haunted Roads and Highways

They say that the journey is just as important, if not more so, than the destination. Well, if the journey is through the commonwealth of Kentucky and the destination is any place other than Kentucky, I am inclined to agree. The scenery through the hills of the Bluegrass State is second to none.

Honestly speaking, as I have traveled America's roads and highways, both in and outside Kentucky, very rarely have I sensed a ghostly presence or, even more rarely, been scared. Rolling along at high rates of speed while focused on traffic safety leaves little room for ghost hunting. The closest thing to driving with spirits I have encountered is falling asleep at the wheel—a very stupid thing to do—and waking up five miles later still perfectly in my lane and still very much alive. I had looked both at the odometer and the lazy full moon in the sky before and after falling asleep. I felt as if a spirit had watched over me as I slept. After I awoke, I quickly pulled to the side of the road to sleep while thanking that gorgeous Cyclops in the night sky for her stewardship. That being said, many have reported spectral encounters along the roads and highways that crisscross our wonderful state. Almost always do they fall into one of two categories: vanishing hitchhikers or bridge visitors. And, statistically speaking, all have their origins due to the death of a traveler—traveling can indeed be a deadly task.

Let's begin by visiting reports of specters as they, in turn, visit the bridges where they met their end.

While researching this first stretch of Kentucky's roadways, I was sidetracked by the subject of covered bridges. These fascinating and beautiful pieces of architecture once traversed thousands of creeks and rivers—over

400 in Kentucky alone. Beginning in the late 1700s, made of wood and stone, covered bridges allowed wagons and animals and people to cross relatively narrow bodies of water, all while staying dry from the rain or snow. Imagine ducking for cover under the wooden beams like today's travelers briefly stopping under concrete overpasses during a torrential downpour or ducking from large hailstones! In many areas, the Civil War took its toll (pardon the pun) on many covered bridges by burning them to ashes and thereby slowing the travel time of the opposing side. Both Confederate and Union armies were guilty of this sin. In Kentucky, only thirteen covered bridges remain, with a mere four allowing vehicular traffic. One of these is the Colville Covered Bridge in Barbour County. All the remaining covered bridges in Kentucky, including the Colville Covered Bridge, are on the National Register of Historic Places.

Colville Covered Bridge
Paris

It's easy to get here. Just follow US 68 through Main Street in Paris, Kentucky, going toward Millersburg (that's northeast for the men reading), turn left at road 1893 (Millersburg Ruddles Mill Road), follow to Colville Road (3118), and turn right. Those directions are from the Kentucky Tourism website.[1] The covered bridge crosses the South Fork of the Licking River.

Easy to get there, as mentioned, but perhaps not so easy to leave! In the 1930s, three people died before they were able to cross. An old woman on her way to the doctor expired before reaching the other side. Several researchers list her name as Sarah Mitchell. Some say that her spirit still cries for help; sounds of coughing or sobbing can be heard at night. A young couple on their way to the prom (a bit urban myth, you say?) crashed through the side and drowned in the waters below. It is this prom couple's demise that has led to reports of sightings of headlights shining up from the river's water at night. The headlights first appear behind you on the bridge, disappear, and then shine up through the bridge's floor from the murky waters below. Eerie!

A number of ghost investigators have visited the site, taking more photos and EVPs than you could shake a dousing rod at. Patti Starr has an excellent chapter in her book *Ghosthunting Kentucky*.[2] Lisa Potts has an entry on her blog—My Haunted Hometown.[3] The bridge even made the short list of only eight states in an article posted to Moviepilot in May 2015 and penned by Sam Warrington.[4]

For the fans of architectural details: The Colville Covered Bridge was built in 1877 by Jacob Bower. The bridge is of a truss design and was first constructed of poplar wood. It is 124 feet long and eighteen feet wide. In 1913, it was restored by Louis Bower. Louis's son, Stock Bower, further restored the bridge and raised it to its current height in 1937. The rough-hewn structure was dismantled in 1997 during its most recent restoration, with the bridge finally reopened to vehicular traffic in 2001.

When you visit, enjoy and appreciate the craftsmanship and beauty of this wonderful bridge . . . and say hello to whatever ghosts you may encounter.

Child's Branch Bridge
Closplint

Off Route 38 in Harlan County, there is a bridge with a rather ominous reputation. Child's Branch Road crosses a section of creek by the same name. The apparition here is no friendly ghost, as she actively tries to cause accidents so that others may join her in the spirit realm. *She* died on the bridge—so why shouldn't you!? In fact, so many accidents with reports of a ghostly woman causing the drivers to crash have occurred that local police have stopped doubting the ghost stories of the drivers. If it happened at night on the bridge . . . a ghost was involved. And the descriptions of the ghost are far from average. Horrific. Terrifying. It is not the attempt to dodge the woman in the road; it is the intense glare of the ghost that penetrates the very soul of the driver that causes the crash.[5]

Middle Bridge Road
Warren County

Another young woman who moved to the other realm due to a car crash now appears from a sudden, inexplicable forming of fog on this bridge at night. Her phantom appears in the fog, an oncoming car gets incapacitated, and she looks inside the car with ghastly eyes. She then disappears, the fog fades, and then the car restarts . . . or so the stories go.[6] The more I looked for evidence of this apparition, the more the story changed.

First, a portion of Middle Bridge Road (before it reaches the bridge) was closed after the flooding on Drake's Creek washed the bridge out some time during the early 1970s. Thus, all those books and websites that listed Middle Bridge as a haunted bridge hadn't checked Google Earth or visited the bridge in person for nearly forty years! A blogger who goes by the name of "Gclee" supplied the following information on his blogsite under the headline "The Legends of Middle Bridge" on October 5, 2013.[7]

Looking for a ghost in the fog on a bridge that no longer exists can be just a tad difficult, so I was glad to find such information before driving through Bowling Green! This excellent blog claims that the Middle Bridge Road (where the bridge once was) is rich in lore and legend. He believes that unusual things have occurred there and continue to happen. He describes the area in this manner:

> The road is now separated into two sections, one on each side of Drake's Creek, and at least half a mile of the old road on the east side has been allowed to grow over, and is now part of farmland. The west part of Middle Bridge Road leaves Lover's Lane near the airport and goes under I-65, ending at Cumberland Trace, which runs parallel with I-65. This particular section is on a hill above Drake's Creek, and where the old Middle Bridge Road went down to the creek has been allowed to grow back to woods, behind the Cumberland Ridge subdivision.

This description is accurate. You can still park your car where Middle Bridge Road ends, and then walk up the remnants of the old road to where the bridge once was. If you have any sensitivity at all to things like this, you will feel something. Things have definitely happened here!

I love detail!

Time changes things. It changes the landscape . . . and it changes the stories that people claim were once historical events. In fact, this Drake's Creek / Middle Bridge area on the outskirts of Bowling Green was once a stagecoach path near the creek and the site of a ferry to cross the creek before Middle Bridge was built.

As far as the ghostly girl legend goes, in the 1920s or '30s a young girl allegedly drowned in Drake's Creek near Middle Bridge. According to this very detail-oriented blogger, she was the sister of Milton Hancock, or "Uncle Milt" as he was known, who operated a nearby BBQ on Cemetery Road. With details such as these, it is not impossible to verify such a tragedy through newspaper stories and obituaries, but I found none.

Twenty to thirty years later (in the 1950s), a story circulated that a young girl had been raped and killed in the area by the bridge, and it is here that the legend of the ghost peering into your car on the bridge began, as if she were looking for those who committed such terrible crimes. The legend: if you park near the bridge, on the east side, the young woman's ghost will travel down the hill, cross the bridge, and approach the car until she finally stops on the hood of the car, glaring through the windshield. Were you her killer? Were you one of those who brutally raped her?

Local residents, however, have the opinion that no girl was ever raped there and that nobody died along Middle Branch Road. Tales persisted and prompted the daring to explore. During the 1960s, two couples, while double-dating, parked near the bridge and claimed to witness a light that settled on the hood of their car. The car immediately began vibrating. When they attempted to start the car, it wouldn't. Only after the light had disappeared for five or ten minutes would the car finally start.

During that same period, three Western Kentucky University professors and a chihuahua that always accompanied one of the men observed the bridge for over a week. Late one night, after several nights of no activity, the dog began shivering and whining. They all then watched the light come down the nearest hill to settle on the hood of the car. The car began vibrating and shaking and then failed to start. They watched the light travel to the bridge before taking the shape of a girl. They each swore this story to be true.

The final ghost sighting to be told was during the late 1980s. A man who worked for the farmer who owned the land off Hunts Lane, where Middle Bridge used to cross the creek, was plowing at night guided by only the headlamps of the tractor when he saw the trees and overgrowth near the creek, where the bridge once was, tossed furiously by the wind. However, all other areas were calm and still. He fled the area never to return. At this time, during the '80s, the ghostly tale was that a young girl had fallen out of the back of a moving car and died right there on the bridge. Obviously, these grown men and women cared little if the light and apparition were from someone who drowned, was raped and murdered, or died from a tragic fall. All they knew was that they saw something out of the ordinary and wanted to flee the area. This is one Kentucky backroad where there is time to explore!

Here one moment, gone the next.

In the next chapter, we will explore another example of what is known as the "vanishing hitchhiker" when we visit "Hot Rod Haven" on the outskirts of Louisville. I include "Resurrection Mary" there due to the fact that such a winding road travels alongside a cemetery. As mentioned, there is often an overlapping as to where to include some entries: dangerous curvy roads, cemeteries, and ghosts go hand in hand.

Here, we will explore the vanishing hitchhiker in more detail with ghosts sighted in Monroe County and the Cane Valley area near Campbellsville.

Meshack Creek Road
Tompkinsville

Running alongside shallow Meshack Creek outside Tompkinsville in Monroe County, Meshack Creek Road has been the site of many instances of an unseen force latching hold of the riders of a horse or motorcycle as they pass a sycamore tree at a sharp bend in the road. It "vanishes" after a mile or so. Such tales have occurred since the late 1950s, leading one to believe that perhaps someone died shortly before that time in an accident at the sycamore. Or perhaps a hanging, and a hitchhiker merely wants to quickly escape the scene?[8]

One version of this legend has a young man picking up a lovely girl dressed in a long gown along this stretch of road one evening. He escorts her to the school dance and drives her home afterward, giving her his jacket to wear to dash through the rain to her front door at the end of a wonderful night. When he returned the next day to retrieve his jacket, the girl's mother reported that the daughter had been gone almost a year and was buried in the nearby graveyard. When the youth visited her final resting place, his jacket was there on the grave![9]

Spooky story, but the whole school dance theme always tends to make me think of an embellishment. Perhaps he thought he saw a pretty young hitchhiker in the rain and added the rest later to impress friends? However, that he saw a vanishing hitchhiker after so many past experiences is completely understandable. Decide for yourself as you travel the fringes of Tomkinsville.

Highway 55
Cane Valley

A more conventional vanishing hitchhiker tale has evolved along the stretches of Highway 55 that run along the western side of Green River Lake near Campbellsville.

Here, a phantom teenaged girl begs for a ride and travels for a while in the passenger seat, only to disappear when she arrives at her destination. This is the classic vanishing-hitchhiker tale. In this example, she wears a wet cotton dress.[10] What is it with young women dying in the rain? And especially on the way to a dance? Perhaps it is the treacherousness of rain-slickened roads and excitable (and distractible) young men driving too fast! A lesson for us all to keep our eyes on the road!

And sometimes young women do not die on the highway but instead are discarded along secluded stretches of road after murderous actions. This brings us to US Highway 25.

Statewide

When locations are mysterious—think of the Bermuda Triangle or Area 51—they tend to accumulate drama . . . such as death . . . such as tragedy . . . that lead to what we know as hauntings. I had come across many references to US Highway 25, so it was not unusual to read of a missing person's cold case solved with the help of the ghost of a young murdered woman, as described in the book *Ghosthunting Kentucky* by Patti Starr.[11] The body of a dead girl, unceremoniously wrapped in a tarp, had been dumped in a gully along US Highway 25N. After the body had been discovered on May 17, 1968, it was taken to St. Joseph's Hospital, in Lexington, for an autopsy. The girl had been struck on the head, tied up, and wrapped in a tarp, where she slowly suffocated, the autopsy revealed. She was buried in a Georgetown cemetery at marker #90—nothing more. Later, local residents placed a headstone with her identifying statistics inscribed under the title "Tent Girl" since she was discovered wrapped in a tarp.

At times, random coincidences and the connections we make during life can lead a person, with a little ghostly help, to feel driven to solve a mystery. The ghost of the tent girl dumped along US Highway 25N began visiting investigator Todd Mathews, whose father-in-law discovered her body twenty years earlier. The mention of that discovery so long ago led to the viewing of her grave marker, which led to a website being established, which in turn led to a family member contacting the investigator—Mr. Mathews. There were ghostly visits and informative dreams along the way until Tent Girl's body was exhumed on March 2, 1998, for DNA analysis. The cold case was solved, with the body being that of Barbara Ann Hackmann-Taylor, who had been missing since late 1967. For an excellent description of the full story, read Patti Starr's chapter titled "Tent Girl."

What an amazing chain of events, and what an amazing example of ghostly activity.

Many roads and stretches of highway gather ghostly tales like a bookshelf gathers dust. And the more tales that accumulate, the more some tales are embellished so that those who travel such routes almost expect to see something ghostly. Every state has many examples of disappearing ghostly hitchhikers, and antigravity hills are everywhere (such as the one at Sparta, Kentucky). They exist in almost all of Kentucky's 120 counties.

US 25 is just such a route. It begins in Covington, at the Cincinnati, Ohio, border, and meanders southward like a snake with nowhere to go, before finally heading into the mountains of Tennessee. If the story of Tent Girl found on US 25N wasn't enough to make you extra cautious as you drive this highway, let's travel in the opposite direction. On US 25S, near, Livingston, Kentucky, there is a sharp curve where a ghostly female hitchhiker seeks to enter your car on a dark night. Along the trip, she will converse and then suddenly fade from view as the road straightens. Many have attempted to give this girl a ride, and then they share their tales with those they trust. Personally, I have driven this stretch of highway several times, mostly during the day, but no visitations have occurred; however, I'm still waiting for the right stretch of road on the right evening to meet just the right girl.[12]

Sparta

Fig. 45: Lost Branch Creek in Sparta, Kentucky.

This spectral sighting is a variation of the vanishing hitchhiker—vanishing handprints.

In the small town of Sparta, Kentucky, tiny ghostly hands just might push your car uphill on KY 465 / Boone Road. Why, you ask? Legend has it that a pioneer boy was startled by "Indians" as he was collecting water at Lost Branch Creek and his wagon rolled backwards, killing him instantly. Thus, he has a habit of pushing vehicles uphill in an attempt to aid them from a fate like his own. But it happens only at dusk and only during the summer.[13] I'm guessing this is when he died. The short stretch of this narrow, two-lane road is called Lost Branch Anti-Gravity Hill and is obviously near the creek. Lost Branch Creek can be seen in figure 45.

The rules: Park at the bottom of the steep hill with your car in neutral, and hold your foot over the brake (for safety). Some have sworn this has happened to them with a slight rolling back. When the pushing has ended, there follows a thump as if a small boy were run over, and finally a painful scream. I believe the scream was an embellishment due to nerves, but you be the judge. As mentioned, this road is steep, narrow, and full of blind curves, so use extreme caution and show courtesy to the few locals who use this public road.

Now that we've traveled roads and highways where many have met their fate, let's visit the cemeteries where they have been placed for all eternity.

Fig. 46: Dangerous curves along KY 465/Boone Road
in Sparta, Kentucky.

> *"My grandfather always said a sudden shiver
> meant someone had just stepped on the spot
> where your grave would be."*
> —Richard Bowes, Weird Detectives: Recent Investigations

CHAPTER FIVE

Haunted Cemeteries

Cemeteries are certainly places where many folks expect to experience ghosts. I, however, have quite mixed feelings regarding such an assumption. Even though cemeteries are filled with history, well-crafted architecture, and often a bounty of natural splendor, they are repositories for the deceased shells of the recently departed. (Figure 47 depicts one example of military history and the wonder of nature reclaiming her own.) People rarely die in a cemetery, and thus their spirits should haunt the location prior to the graveyard, where

Fig. 47: Nature reclaims her own in Cave Hill
Cemetery, Louisville, Kentucky.

their trauma or confusion was experienced. That being said, cemeteries, as the final resting place of physical remains, might very well act as the highway between the living and the dead, and there are seemingly countless tales of spectral activity within cemeteries, with sightings occurring quite regularly.

In southwestern Jefferson County, on the outskirts of Louisville and just a few miles from the Waverly Hills Sanatorium, two cemeteries wait at the crest of two winding and deadly roads. There are legends surrounding each. The first, a private cemetery for several local families, most notably the Griffen and Mitchell families, is located at 1309 Mitchell Hill Road. Over the years, more than twenty-five souls have met their fates on the twisting road, which hosts a straightaway that suddenly makes a sharp left turn toward eternity. One unfortunate tragedy grew into the legend of "Hotrod Haven" and one of many variations of the Resurrection Mary story. In this case, sometime around 1950, a young woman and her date were on their way to a dance, maybe the prom, when they were killed at the bottom of Mitchell Hill Road in a car crash. Since then, many have reported seeing a young woman in a party dress wandering along the road and looking forlorn and lost in the cemetery at the top of the hill. The legend continues that she and her young lover were buried in that small hilltop cemetery.

Many have called this ghostly figure "Mary" or "Sarah," with the name of the male long forgotten or never known. In September 2000, fifty years after the legend began, Louisville ghost researcher Keith Age retraced the route of the two teenagers of that fateful evening. Before driving Mitchell Hill Road and walking through the small hilltop burial ground, he discovered Jefferson County records listing the deaths of Sarah Mitchell and Roy Clarke on September 23, 1946, resulting from a car crash as they traveled to a school dance. Clarke had lost control on the curve, and both were pronounced dead at the scene. Mr. Age reported the discovery of a single headstone with

Fig. 48: Family cemetery on Mitchell Hill Road in Louisville.

two names etched side by side: Sarah Mitchell . . . Roy Clarke, September 23, 1946, as he investigated in 2000.[1]

However, my visit in April 2015 revealed no Sarah Mitchell or Roy Clarke on any stone in the small graveyard. All other descriptions still apply. Check for yourself. Oftentimes, after stories appear in print or video, graveyards are disturbed and headstones are stolen or damaged. This is a small and beautiful cemetery, so please treat it with respect. From the top of the hill the sounds of vehicles and animals can echo from miles away, and there is also quite a view. However, be careful as you drive, since Sarah may want a ride to find her Roy and finally escape "Hotrod Haven."

St. Andrew Catholic Cemetery
Louisville

A second cemetery in southwestern Jefferson County also has a Resurrection Mary story with yet another young couple meeting an untimely end. This time the road is St. Anthony Church Road and the cemetery is the St. Andrew Catholic Cemetery, located at 7306 Rica Road. The legend goes that a young man and woman were headed to a dance when their car ran out of gas (Why is dancing so dangerous in these stories?). The young man went off alone in search of gas along the winding roads at night in the direction of the cemetery. When her boyfriend did not return in a reasonable amount of time, she went in search of her lover. What she saw so terrified her, the legend reports, that she returned screaming to their car and hanged herself from the branch of a roadside tree where their car had stalled.

At some point in time, someone painted a devil on this tree, and the many attempts to remove or cover the devil's face were all in vain as the devil showed his face through the paint time and time again; this tree was dubbed, of course, "The Devil Tree." Many have claimed to have seen the young woman on subsequent nights as she searched for her lost lover, while others have claimed to have seen her ghost dangling from the ill-fated tree. Only recently has a chainsaw finally erased the devil's grin—"The Devil Tree" was deemed a hazard too close to the twisting curves of St. Anthony Church Road. This is yet another example of history and legend being lost in the name of "progress."

Figure 49 shows the fearless author smiling like the devil in 2007, before "The Devil Tree" finally lost its grin. St. Andrew Catholic Cemetery at the top of the hill has also been the site of reported ghostly sightings both of the young woman and the young man.

Fig. 49: Author poses beside the "Devil Tree," a legend
within a legend. *Courtesy of Christopher Meyer.*

Was this an actual couple? Are they buried in St. Andrew Catholic Cemetery? How did the young man die and what was so terrifying to his girlfriend?

I went searching for signs of an actual couple within the graveyard in early 2007, along with my son. What followed us around through the cemetery was not an apparition, but rather the sound of a small bell that moved along with us just out of reach. We never caught up to the bell, and there was no cat or other animal that could have eluded our sighting so consistently and for so long. In centuries past, when medical science was not as precise as it is today, people were buried with a bell in their caskets just in case they were buried while still alive. Edgar Allan Poe's "The Premature Burial," first published in 1844, describes just such an experience. Was this ringing bell telling us that someone died before their time?

The boundaries which divide Life from Death are at best shadowy and vague. Who shall say where the one ends, and where the other begins?

—Edgar Allan Poe, "The Premature Burial"

Cave Hill Cemetery
Louisville

Established in 1848, Cave Hill Cemetery is one of the most beautiful cemeteries in the state, if not the country. It is the final resting place of many historical and famous individuals—so many in fact that there are many volumes both on the history as well as its scenic beauty. For that reason, I will keep this entry brief because I cannot adequately cover all the wonderful qualities of this cemetery in a few short pages. I will summarize the wonder with a few lines from a blog entry called "Telling the Stories of the Dead: Louisville's Cave Hill Cemetery," written by Nancy McCabe:

I begin to notice birds everywhere: the grave of a pet bird named Pretty Polly, a tarnished St. Francis leaning out from beneath an arch, releasing a dove. An actual robin landing on a stone, ducks and geese loitering on the road, sparrows in the maples and dogwoods. A polished gravestone rising out of natural rock, topped with wrought iron hawks frozen in the act of lifting off. "They will soar on wings of eagles," says the Kessler family stone, a quote from Isaiah.

But the one place where you might expect to find birds—the grave of Kentucky Fried Chicken magnate "Colonel" Sanders—is noticeably absent of a wrought

Fig. 50: World famous Colonel Harland Sanders, creator of Kentucky Fried Chicken. His final resting place is within Cave Hill Cemetery in Louisville.

iron or stained glass or marble or bronze chicken, instead displaying a bust of Harland Sanders. In a poem carved on a stone nearby, his daughter Margaret compares herself not to a bird but to a "ballet dancer/poised briefly with just the tip of one toe/to the earth."

These objects—a baseball, a swing set, a hawk, a dancer's toe—can't fully capture the complexity of a life, but there's something touching about the effort. As these monuments search for the one perfect image to compact experience and personalities, to pinpoint what is ultimately elusive, they nevertheless offer starting points from which whole stories can unfold.[2]

Defining life or our acceptance of death is a difficult task. There is so much history here . . . and raw emotion . . . it is not surprising that many ghost stories also inhabit this very large cemetery (297 acres). A few of the many spectral reports include green lights that hover over tombstones, the chanting of church hymns under a full moon, and even the apparition of Colonel Sanders himself!

However, even if you never see a ghost, hear eerie chants or bump into a deceased icon, a day here is a day among treasures that will haunt your memory for the rest of your life. For the living . . . the cemetery is open 8:00 a.m. to 4:45 p.m. with the main entrance located at 701 Baxter Avenue. I've walked through this cemetery a hundred times, and I eagerly look forward to the next visit! It never grows old.

Let's travel a bit southeast, approximately forty miles as the crow flies, to another hotspot of Kentucky's haunted cemeteries—Bardstown, Kentucky.

Pioneer Cemetery
Bardstown

Bardstown has more than its fair share of haunted places (two haunted inns were examined in a previous chapter), and now we will explore two haunted cemeteries. The first, Pioneer Cemetery (see the historical marker, figure 51), conveniently waits directly behind what is currently the Jailer's Inn but was a working jail for 168 years, with the site used for the detainment of prisoners from 1797 through 1987, as described earlier. Numerous prisoners were hanged or otherwise died at the jail, including Martin Hill, who was convicted of murdering his wife in 1885 but died in horrible pain before his hanging could occur.

Many have claimed to have seen or heard an otherworldly Mr. Hill screeching in pain around the grounds. I mention it here because it is so convenient to have a cemetery located so close to where people die, and, for

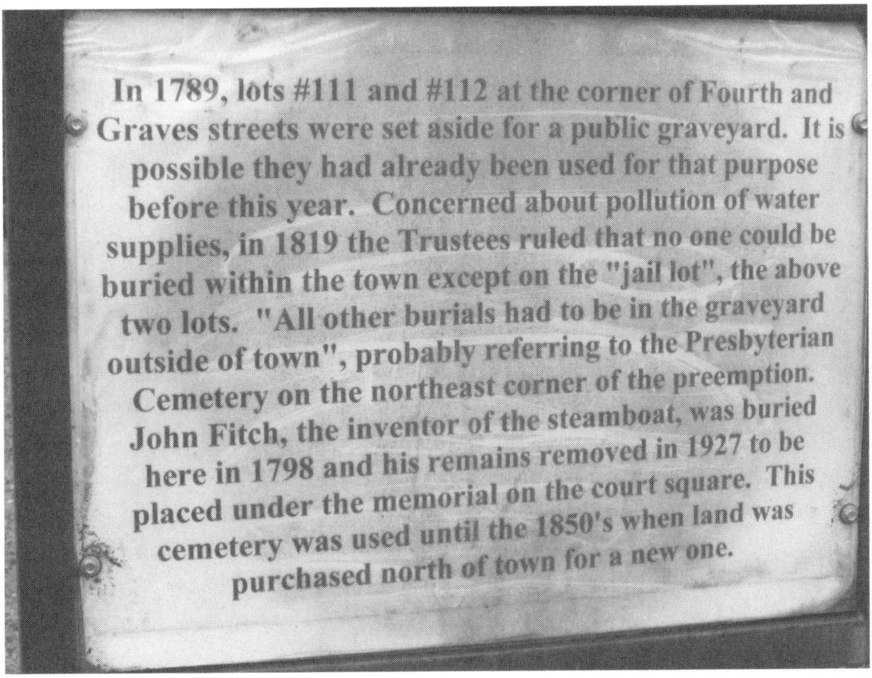

In 1789, lots #111 and #112 at the corner of Fourth and Graves streets were set aside for a public graveyard. It is possible they had already been used for that purpose before this year. Concerned about pollution of water supplies, in 1819 the Trustees ruled that no one could be buried within the town except on the "jail lot", the above two lots. "All other burials had to be in the graveyard outside of town", probably referring to the Presbyterian Cemetery on the northeast corner of the preemption. John Fitch, the inventor of the steamboat, was buried here in 1798 and his remains removed in 1927 to be placed under the memorial on the court square. This cemetery was used until the 1850's when land was purchased north of town for a new one.

Fig. 51: Cemetery marker in Pioneer Cemetery, Bardstown, Kentucky.

the purposes of the discussion of ghosts, where people are "killed"! Why shouldn't there be spirits shocked into haunting this cemetery . . . and why shouldn't visitors hear and see unexplainable things!?

The graveyard contains various historical markers, including that of John Fitch, steamboat inventor, who was buried here from 1798 until 1927, when his remains were exhumed to be reinterred at a monument on Courtyard Square. The digging up of a person's remains is yet another plausible explanation for a haunting!

More than one person has seen and heard a ghostly black cat in Pioneer Cemetery. It appears from a broken crypt and disappears as you exit the graveyard, and it has been sighted for a span of time far beyond what cats usually exist. Some say this is a ghostly guardian of the cemetery. Some say that a spirit once interred in one of the graves has entered the body of a cat (or cats). Some say it is the spirit of a woman accused of witchcraft and hanged nearby.[3] Who is to say which is right or wrong? But if you see a black cat in the cemetery under a full moon . . . watch closely!

Bardstown Cemetery
Bardstown

Ignore the wishes of the dead and see what you get! Before his death on July 13, 1843, Senator John Rowan forbade that any stone or monument be placed on his grave. He was, after all, a humble man. However, after his relatives ignored such a directive by placing a large marker over his final resting place, things began to happen. Within a few months, the tall grave marker within Bardstown Cemetery on US 31E/150 began toppling from its base for no explainable reason. Frightened stonemasons, after attempting to replace the marker, refused to return to the cemetery.[4]

Visit the tall obelisk with its stone wreath and carved list of Rowan's accomplishments, if you dare. Is it standing? Just down the road at 501 E. Stephen Foster Avenue is the senator's former home—Federal Hill—where his cousin, Stephen Collins Foster, wrote the Kentucky standard "My Old Kentucky Home." Is the song playing in your head as you read this? A haunting melody, isn't it? History, as well, haunts us all if we choose to walk along those darkened, lonely paths.

From Bardstown, let's travel a couple or three hours and a couple of hundred miles westward to the city of Paducah.

Fig. 52: Tombstones in Bardstown Cemetery.

Fig. 53: A cherubic angel watches over
Bardstown Cemetery.

Lone Oak German Cemetery
Paducah

This cemetery is one of the most atmosphere-laden cemeteries that I have ever encountered. It screams "haunt me" from every tombstone, and I wish I could include a dozen photos just from this single location. The legends here include a "werewolf"-type creature that charges up the hill at visitors, a female apparition that harbors a grudge toward members of the male gender, and a strange light that hovers over a single grave in the lower portion of the cemetery. It has been reported that even the crickets are silenced when such visitations occur.[5]

Located across from St. John's Catholic Church on St. John's Church Road, this small cemetery rests atop a steep incline that puts the deceased

Fig. 54: Lone Oak German Cemetery with St. John's Catholic Church in the background—Paducah, Kentucky. This boneyard has it all—a werewolf, ghostly lights, and man-hating spirits.

atop a perch overlooking the church and the hilly roads that run parallel and perpendicular to this parcel of land that blends mystery and beauty. As you move away from the road and the church, the cemetery slopes rapidly downhill toward wooded areas on the other three sides, making the cemetery completely hidden from prying eyes.

During my visit, a large dog howled and barked from somewhere nearby. This fact, and the secluded nature of the cemetery, explains much of the "werewolf" legend. Perhaps at some point, a large dog or coyote emerged from the woods on an unsuspecting visitor . . . under a full moon . . . on a crisp autumn evening shrouded with fog. Even if the canine meant no harm, I can see such an action amid the secluded and unfamiliar terrain causing even a calm soul to run from the area, thinking notions of lycanthropy

Fig. 55: Nearly gone . . . and almost forgotten?

and silver bullets. The apparition of a woman with a dislike toward men may be explained by a simple walk through the cemetery. One of the sad facts of life regarding graveyards is that as the decades turn to centuries, they fall into disrepair. Many of the grave markers here have fallen over or been vandalized so that they are lying on the ground broken or recessing into the earth, where they are overlooked and forgotten. There are no flowers . . . no visitors . . . no memories . . . no love . . . just loneliness and a collection of past lives that have given way to a present where history and legacy are all but forgotten. Many of the broken headstones and monuments belong to women, as are many of the markers that are barely visible among the dirt and are soon to be lost to the ages.

Even the strange light in the lower portion of the graveyard may have a logical, if not overly psychological, explanation. At the lower left corner of the cemetery and far removed from all the other graves is a single marker

Fig. 56: A single and isolated grave at the back of
Lone Oak German Cemetery. Valid reasons?

belonging to James and John Jennings. These two brothers died young; James
at twenty-four years of age, which was common in the mid-nineteenth century.
The only thing that truly separates these two men from the other inhabitants
is that the Jennings brothers were born in Ireland while the lion's share, if not
all, of the cemetery's other occupants were born in Germany or came from
German stock. Were there plans to inter other Irish men and women here and
the Jenningses' burials were just the result of unfortunate timing . . . or were
these two men made an example as not fitting in? To put it simply: Were they
ostracized for all eternity on purpose or merely by mistake?

As far as the strange light is concerned, anyone knowing there is a single
tomb far removed from all the others must wonder and hold reservations in
the back of their minds about the reason why. This grave is also the one nearest
to a neighboring parcel of land with a long white fence and electric lights
that dance among the foliage as the wind blows.

And . . . in the midst of all this death and forgotten history, there is beauty
and the renewal of life!

Fig. 57: Nature and beauty make death less heartbreaking.

Fig. 58: Comfort to the living and the dead.

Oak Grove Cemetery
Paducah

Located in the heart of Paducah, at 1613 Park Avenue, Oak Grove Cemetery offers beautiful natural settings, the inclusion of historical figures, and ghostly legends. Paducah native John T. Scopes, of the famous Scopes Monkey Trial, was interred here in 1970. In violation of the Tennessee law that forbade the teaching of Charles Darwin's theory of evolution, twenty-four-year-old biology teacher Scopes was charged and went to trial in 1925. He was convicted and fined $100. The law was repealed in Tennessee in 1967 . . . three years before he died.

Dr. Reuben Saunders, credited with the discovery that the hypodermic use of morphine-atropine halted cholera during the 1873 epidemic, was also

Fig. 59: Oak Grove Cemetery entry marker.

laid to eternal rest here on these grounds in 1891. He was responsible for telegraphing this prescription to other plague-stricken areas and thus saved many lives.

The grave markers of these two historic figures have not seen a fraction of the drama given to young Della Robinson Barnes, whose restless spirit is said to continue to walk the many paths of Oak Grove Cemetery. Della, the daughter of George F. Barnes and Anna M. Robinson, died of an accidental poisoning in 1897. The *Paducah Sun-Democrat* reported that twenty-two-year-old Della had died an "accidental death...Morphine taken for Calomel." However, a second telling of her death reports something very different . . . and more ghastly. Della, engaged to a prominent local businessman, had fallen for another, less wealthy, man. Her wealthy fiancée, hearing of her rejection, cut off her slender finger to retrieve the engagement ring, and she promptly bled to death.

Over the years the life-sized marble statue that marked Della's grave was said to cry real tears and bleed from her fingertips. In fact, vandals broke her left-hand ring finger off and kept it so that her blood could more easily flow. Later, vandals broke off the head of the statue and removed the head from the grounds. The body of the statue was toppled to the ground so many times that it is now in storage at the cemetery, with no marker whatsoever signifying the earth above Della Barnes's remains.

Her mother and father are also without markers at the family plot, located in the Old Section 9, 136. There is a stain on a neighboring mausoleum that

Fig. 60: Even eyes of stone can't bear to witness
the sadness. Grave marker at Oak Grove
Cemetery in Paducah, Kentucky.

is rumored to be the shadow of Della's grave marker. On certain nights, the ghost of Della Barnes is said to walk along the path at Oak Grove. The angel marker on the grave of Nannie Barber (1845–1895), shown in figure 60, is said to turn her head to look away from the sadness of Della's restless spirit.

If you would like a very detailed and interesting article describing the history of Della Barnes and calling for the restoration of her grave marker, follow the link included in the endnotes.[6]

Figure 61 depicts more decapitated grave markers, this time of a mother and her children. A close examination of the statues that mark the graves of Dasha Wilcox (1855–1888) and her two little girls (both died under the age of three) reveals missing heads and broken left ankles. Why are only the statues of young women being decapitated? Are their necks merely more slender, thus making this a natural occurrence? Or is there more to it—natural or unnatural? This is both sad and disturbing.

Fig. 61: Headless mother and child at Oak Grove Cemetery, Paducah.

Figures 62 and 63 show another grave marker for a young woman . . . this time with a head! The right side of her face is both intact and beautiful; however, the left side of her face has been worn by weather and time to a point where she is nearly unrecognizable. Figure 64 shows a three-legged bench that perhaps waits for a headless woman or child, or even as a resting spot for Della Barnes to find a moment's peace along her eternal wandering.

Oak Grove Cemetery is managed by the Paducah Parks Services Department. The cemetery has an estimated 35,278 platted lots with more than 33,000 sold. The cemetery is divided into four additions: Old, New, Mausoleum, and Rushing. Please use the information below to schedule appointments for tours or to inquire about services.

Traveling back east, let's visit a couple of small cemeteries in a couple of small towns. Ghosts, after all, are nondiscriminatory!

Fig. 62: Two-faced grave marker.

Fig. 63: The effects of time and weather.

Fig. 64: A three-legged bench at the back of the photo to rest upon while visiting.

Ridge Cemetery
Glasgow

Sometimes legends require a stretch of the imagination to connect the dots. An argument that led to two brothers killing each other (the perfectly timed firing of two pistols?) in this cemetery, in the 1880s, caused them to haunt this land. So the story goes. They make their presence known by ringing a tiny bell.[7] I've heard this bell sound in other cemeteries—but not here. Remember the premature burial that Mr. Poe was so fond of?

This graveyard is north of Glasgow in Barron County.

Grandview Cemetery
Elizabethtown

This cemetery, about eighteen miles west of Elizabethtown at the end of St. John Road, is also known as Kasey's Cemetery (there's a stone sign on the ground) or "The Gates of Hell." This last foreboding moniker began, some say, when the old wooden sign was set on fire by vandals. Others report "satanic" rituals having occurred here, while still others say that witches have had their rituals here and even that some were hanged on the property. Still others speak of a boy who was hanged, and they point to a low branch from a tree near the rear of the graveyard. None of these accusations have evidence to support them. There's lots of talk, obviously, and one thing's for sure: teenagers have hung out here, drinking and vandalizing the old tombstones. This is a sad fact since many of the graves are from the 1800s and are important to the family members of the deceased. One newspaper article described the dumping of animal carcasses on the property.[8]

Ghostly reports have been made of an enormous green orb that hovered above a grave before shooting into the sky and disappearing. Others speak of screams and shadow figures in addition to inexplicable car troubles and batteries being drained of their energy.[9] Many of these may owe their existence to the actions of the aforementioned teenagers. However, paranormal investigators have produced EVPs and other phenomena. One thing should be understood here: Be careful should you visit this property. There is a caretaker nearby who reports suspicious activity to local law enforcement. As always—respect the property of the living and the dead.

Conclusion

I want to thank you for taking this journey with me through haunted halls and attics, hills and valleys, and winding trails, paved and otherwise, across our beautiful and historic commonwealth of Kentucky. These destinations are best when they are shared, and it is perhaps that very reason why ghosts persist in our material world. If you were not a believer before, I sincerely hope that I have broadened your horizons if only by the slightest of margins—a cracked door through which to spy on another realm, whether it be intellectual or spiritual. And if you were a believer before—I trust I have led you down some new paths to further explore the world where ghosts remain rooted to their origins.

Here, I want to leave a summary of main points I have discussed in the preceding chapters. First and foremost, enter each and every location—whether it is a crumbling 200-year-old farmhouse or a bright, sunlit meadow—with an open mind that is both skeptical and accepting. Use good judgment. Believe in the goodness and pureness of your heart . . . that your moral compass is strong enough to counter any and every force. The unknown is nothing to fear, yet a respect toward all things, seen and unseen, must be present. And above all, trust your instincts.

Often, people have preconceived notions that let fear creep in where none is necessary. This fear leads to a lack of trust and often to a misinterpretation. If a written sign or a person warns of "evil," use caution yet understand that past reports may simply have been based on misunderstanding and misplaced fear. I will repeat—I have never encountered anything malicious or dangerous in the world of spirits or hauntings. It has always been a bridge to understanding and an appreciation of the unknown.

Many, if not most, tales of hauntings can be explained by misinterpreting natural phenomena, such as knocking pipes, temperature changes in wood or metal, or sights or sounds that become distorted in unfamiliar surroundings. However, ghostly occurrences *do* exist. I have encountered many, and I genuinely look forward to the next . . . and the next . . . and the next.

Many people ask me about my favorite haunting—and my reply is always something along the line of "those where the encounter leads to a greater understanding or a greater peace." The hauntings I dread most are those that leave me emotionally drained because the feelings are so strong, even overwhelming—sadness . . . loneliness . . . confusion. I use only my emotions and a camera to explore—on rare occasions I use an EVP recorder. I speak aloud and with my mind. Remember, TALK to ghosts as if they are there. If not—how can you expect them to communicate with you. Use simple directives so their energies are not exhausted. Orbs, as I have said, are usually dust mites or insects. If they defy the laws of physics and act like a jet pilot, then they just might be something more. When awakening from sleep, dreams seem real. Make sure you are awake before you claim an otherworldly journey as Ebenezer Scrooge did!

This is also an excellent opportunity to plead for the preservation of historical places. Remember, if there is no history, then there are no ghosts. We all need a place to hang our hat! Respect the homes of the dead and the living—gravestones, old houses, and forests dark and deep all provide shelter of one kind or another.

There are many other haunted spots in Kentucky. I have chosen a few that fall into five categories only: restaurants, hotels and inns, parks and natural areas, roads and highways, and cemeteries. There are many others for each of these categories. And there are other categories as well . . . and some that are known worldwide among ghost hunters. I have discussed two—Mammoth Cave and Bobby Mackey's Music World—that have reputations for being haunted. A third, however, did not fit snugly into the chapters of this book. Nonetheless, I would be neglectful if I did not at least mention one of the most haunted places of all time: the Waverly Hills Sanatorium in southwestern Jefferson County, Louisville. I grew up just a few blocks from the former tuberculosis sanatorium and explored the woods behind the behemoth structure as a teen and dared to ride my bicycle up the snakelike road that led to the main entrance. I have tales, as do many, many others . . . of room 502 . . . of Timmy and his leather ball . . . of shadow people . . . of the morgue . . . of the death chute . . . of hangings and dead nurses . . . of disembodied footprints in the dust. The owners give tours and have high hopes for restoration. It is a gem among gems—even if still in the rough.

There are things I have missed, I'm sure, but not for lack of trying! And you will miss them also if you don't explore these and other Kentucky haunts.

The next few pages provide names and other information so that you may continue your journey. Have fun and tell them Dan said hello.

Places to See

Bardstown
(Nelson Co.)

Jailer's Inn (chapter two)
111 W. Stephen Foster Avenue, Bardstown, KY 40004
502-348-5551
www.jailersinn.com

Talbott Tavern (chapter two)
107 W. Stephen Foster Avenue, Bardstown, KY 40004
502-348-3494
www.talbotts.com

Bardstown Cemetery (chapter five)
800 block of North 3rd Street, Bardstown, KY 40004
www.cityofbardstown.org/dept-cemetery

Pioneer Cemetery (chapter five)
East side of 4th Street, Bardstown, KY 40004

Bellevue
(Campbell Co.)

Christopher's Bed and Breakfast (chapter two)
604 Poplar Street, Bellevue, KY 41073
859-491-9354
www.christophersbb.com

Berea
(Madison Co.)

Boone Tavern (chapter one)
100 Main Street North, Berea, KY 40403
800-678-8946
www.boonetavernhotel.com

Bloomfield
(Nelson Co.)

Springhill Plantation Bed and Breakfast (chapter two)
3205 Springfield Road, Bloomfield, KY 40008
502-252-9463
www.springhillwinery.com

Bowling Green
(Warren Co.)

Middle Bridge Road (chapter four)

Brandenburg
(Meade Co.)

Doe Run Inn (chapter one—Odds & Ends)
500 Doe Run Hotel Road, Brandenburg, KY 40108
Note: CLOSED at the time of this writing. Trespassers are subject to local and state laws.

Jailhouse Pizza (chapter one)
125 Main Street, Brandenburg, KY 40108
270-422-4660
www.jailhousepizza.com

Campbellsville
(Taylor Co.)

Tebbs Bend–Green River Bridge Battlefield
(chapter three—Odds & Ends)
2218 Tebbs Bend Road, Campbellsville, KY 42718
270-789-3025
www.tebbsbend.com/history/green-river-bridge

Cane Valley
(Adair Co.)

Highway 55 (chapter four)

Closplint
(Harlan Co.)

Child's Branch Bridge (chapter four)
Route 38

Corbin
(Whitley and Knox Cos.)

Cumberland Falls State Resort Park (chapter three)
7351 KY-90, Corbin, KY 40701
606-528-4121
www.parks.ky.gov/parks/resortparks/cumberland-falls

Elizabethtown
(Hardin Co.)

Old Bethlehem Academy (chapter one—Odds & Ends)
Bethlehem Academy Road, Elizabethtown, KY 42701
Note: CLOSED at the time of this writing. Trespassers are subject to local
and state laws.

Grandview Cemetery / Gates of Hell Cemetery / Kasey Cemetery (chapter five)
Old Hardinsburg Road, Elizabethtown, KY 42701
Note: Latitude: 38.8881219°N, Longitude: 84.255769°W

Georgetown
(Scott Co.)

The Studio (former Lock and Key Café) (chapter one—Odds & Ends)
201 E. Main Street, Georgetown, KY 40324
Note: This location is a massage therapist business. Make contact only if you have the need of a massage therapist.

Glasgow
(Barren Co.)

Ridge Cemetery (chapter five—Odds & Ends)
North of Glasgow, KY 42141

Harrodsburg
(Mercer Co.)

Old Fort Harrod State Park (chapter three)
100 S. College Street, Harrodsburg, KY 40330
859-734-3314
www.parks.ky.gov/parks/recreationparks/fort-harrod

Young Park (chapter three)
546 Linden Ave, Harrodsburg, KY 40330

Lexington
(Fayette Co.)

Campbell House (chapter two)
1375 S. Broadway, Lexington, KY 40504
859-255-4281
www.thecampbellhouse.com

Gratz Park Inn (chapter two)
120 W. 2nd Street, Lexington, KY 40507
859-231-1777
www.gratzparkinn.com

Griffin Gate Marriott Resort & Spa (chapter two)
1800 Newtown Pike, Lexington, KY 40511
859-231-5100
www.marriott.com/hotels/travel/lexky-griffin-gate-marriott-resort-and-spa

London
(Laurel Co.)

Camp Wildcat Battlefield (chapter three—Odds & Ends)
Wildcat Mountain
www.wildcatbattlefield.org/visit.html
Note: Latitude: 37.26528°N, Longitude: 84.20139°W
Destination is at the end of a narrow gravel road. Check website for directions and other information.

Louisville
(Jefferson Co.)

Café 360 (chapter one)
1582 Bardstown Road, Louisville, KY 40205
502-473-8694
Note: Open 24 hours.

Captain's Quarters (chapter one)
5700 Captains Quarters Road, Prospect, KY 40059
502-228-1651
www.cqriverside.com

Cherry Springs/Funk House/Dillon Steakhouse (chapter one—Odds & Ends)
2101 S. Hurstbourne Parkway, Louisville, KY 40220
Note: All food establishments have been permanently closed at this address. It is currently a car lot.

Corbett's: An American Place (chapter one)
5050 Norton Healthcare Boulevard, Louisville, KY 40241
502-327-5058
www.corbettsrestaurant.com (Closed at the time of this writing.)

Derby City Antique Mall (chapter one)
3819 Bardstown Road, Louisville, KY 40218
502-459-5151
www.derbycityantiquemall.com

Highlands Tap Room Grill (chapter one)
1056 Bardstown Road, Louisville, KY 40204
502-584-5222
www.highlandstaproom.com

John E's Restaurant (chapter one—Odds & Ends)
3708 Bardstown Road, Louisville, KY 40218
Note: This restaurant has been completely demolished. The Hikes Family Cemetery remains next to where the cabin/ restaurant once stood.

Mark's Feed Store (chapter one)
1514 Bardstown Road, Louisville, KY 40205
502-458-1570
www.marksfeedstore.com

Phoenix Hill Tavern (chapter one—Odds & Ends)
644 Baxter Avenue, Louisville, KY 40204
Note: Current construction project underway at the time of this writing.

The Brown Hotel (chapter two)
335 W. Broadway, Louisville, KY 40202
502-583-1234
www.brownhotel.com

The Seelbach Hotel (chapter two)
500 South 4th Street, Louisville, KY 40202
502-585-3200
www.seelbachhilton.com

George Rogers Clark Park (chapter three)
1024 Thruston Avenue, Louisville, KY 40217
502-456-8100
www.louisvilleky.gov/government/parks/park-list/george-rogers-clark-park
Note: Park is open from dawn to dusk.

Cave Hill Cemetery (chapter five)
701 Baxter Avenue, Louisville, KY 40204
502-451-5630
www.cavehillcemetery.com

Mitchell Hill Road Cemetery (chapter five)
1309 Mitchell Hill Road, Louisville, KY 40118
Confluence of Mitchell Hill Road, Top Hill Road, and Knob Creek Road
Note: This is a small family cemetery in a residential area. Show respect and tread softly.

St. Andrews Cemetery (chapter five)
7500 Saint Anthonys Church Road, Louisville, KY 40214
502-935-1223
www.stpaulparishlouisvilleky.org

Waverly Hills Tuberculosis Sanatorium (conclusion)
4400 Paralee Lane, Louisville, KY 40272
502-933-2142
www.therealwaverlyhills.com
Note: Except for the tours, this site has strict security due to the excessive vandalism over the years. Make contact before you arrive.

(Edmonson Co.)

Mammoth Cave National Park (chapter three)
1 Mammoth Cave Parkway, Mammoth Cave, KY 42259
270-758-2180
www.nps.gov/maca
Note: Managed by National Park Service.

Mount Olivet
(Robertson Co.)

Blue Licks Battlefield State Park (chapter three—Odds & Ends)
10299 Maysville Road, Carlisle, KY 40311
859-289-5507
www.parks.ky.gov/parks/resortparks/blue_licks

Nancy
(Pulaski Co.)

Millsprings Battlefield (chapter three—Odds & Ends)
Nancy, KY 42544
606-636-4045
www.millsprings.net

Paducah
(McCracken Co.)

Shandies Restaurant (chapter one)
202 Broadway Street, Paducah, KY 42001
270-442-2552
www.m.mainstreethub.com/shandies

Lone Oak German Cemetery (chapter five)
Mayfield Road across from St. John's Catholic Church, Paducah, KY 42001

Oak Grove Cemetery (chapter five)
1613 Park Avenue
Paducah, KY 42001
270-444-8532
www.paducahky.gov/oak-grove-cemetery

Paris
(Bourbon Co.)

Colville Covered Bridge (chapter four)
Route 3118

Perryville
(Boyle Co.)

Perryville Battlefield State Historic Site (chapter three)
1825 Battlefield Road, Perryville, KY 40468
859-332-8631
www.parks.ky.gov/parks/historicsites/perryville-battlefield

Prestonsburg
(Floyd Co.)

Jenny Wiley State Resort Park (chapter three)
75 Theatre Court, Prestonsburg, KY 41653
606-889-1790
www.parks.ky.gov/parks/resortparks/jenny-wiley

Middle Creek National Battlefield (chapter three—Odds & Ends)
KY-114, Prestonsburg, KY 41653
www.middlecreek.org

River
(Johnson Co.)

Jenny Wiley gravesite (chapter three)
Hwy. 581 (by River Volunteer Fire Company)
Note: Open dawn to dusk.

Slade
(Powell Co.)

Natural Bridge State Resort Park (chapter three)
2135 Natural Bridge Road, Slade, KY 40376
606-663-2214
www.parks.ky.gov/parks/resortparks/natural-bridge

Sparta
(Gallatin Co.)

KY 465 (chapter four)

Springfield
(Washington Co.)

Historic Maple Hill Manor Bed & Breakfast (chapter three)
2941 Perryville Road, Springfield, KY 40069
800-886-7546
www.maplehillmanor.com

Statewide
(through many counties)

US Highway 25 (chapter four)

Tompkinsville
(Monroe Co.)

Meshack Creek Road (chapter four)

West Point

(Hardin Co.)

Young House (chapter three—Odds & Ends)
204 Elm Street, West Point, KY 40177
Note: As of this writing, this is a private residence. No trespassing. The property owners deserve respect and privacy. Do not leave the public roadway, and limit photography to daytime/nonflash only.

Wickliffe

(Ballard Co.)

Wickliffe Mounds (chapter three)
94 Green Street, Wickliffe, KY 42087
270-335-3681
www.parks.ky.gov/parks/historicsites/wickliffe-mounds

Wilder

(Campbell Co.)

Bobby Mackey's Music World (chapter one)
44 Licking Pike, Wilder, KY 41071
859-431-5588
www.bobbymackey.com
Note: This facility has posted warnings regarding potential harm from spirits/ghosts. Use good judgment and caution.

Endnotes

Chapter One

1. http://kentuckyghosts.blogspot.com/2013/05/the-ghost-at-cc-cohen.html.
2. https://www.youtube.com/watch?v=-y8M15USKs0.
3. http://jailhousepizza.com/history.html.
4. http://bobbymackey.com/Paranormal/Paranormal.html.
5. http://doubtfulnews.com/2015/04/haunted-history-of-bobby-mackeys-music-world-fails-to-stand-up-to-scrutiny/.
6. www.corbettsrestaurant.com/content/index.php?option=com_content&view=article&id=58&Itemid=53.
7. www.cqriverside.com/about-us/our-history/.
8. http://digital.library.louisville.edu/cdm/ref/collection/potter/id/8.
9. www.leoweekly.com/2008/08/haunted-house-clancy-lowers-the-boom/.
10. www.louisvillehotbytes.com/can-riviera-maya-exorcise-a-haunted-venue.
11. www.strangeusa.com/ViewLocation.aspx?id=64524&desc=_Parisian_Pantry__Louisville__KY&x=1.
12. www.marksfeedstore.com.
13. Holland, Jeffrey Scott. *Weird Kentucky*. New York: Sterling, 2008, p. 193.
14. www.wdrb.com/story/10389992/funk-family-bands-together-to-save-cemetery.

Chapter Two

1. Brown, Alan. *Stories from the Haunted South*. Jackson: University Press of Mississippi, 2004, pp. 98–99.
2. Ibid.
3. Smith, Sarah Borders. Old Talbott Tavern NRHP Nomination Form (Kentucky Heritage Commission, 1972), p. 2.
4. Holland, Jeffrey Scott. *Weird Kentucky*. New York: Sterling, 2008), p. 195.
5. Ibid., p. 197.
6. Starr, Patti. *Ghosthunting Kentucky*. Cincinnati, OH: Clerisy, 2010, pp. 127–128.
7. www.jailersinn.com/#HISTORY.
8. http://theresashauntedhistoryofthetri-state.blogspot.com/2011/05/jailers-inn-bardstown-ky.html.

9. www.hauntedplaces.org/item/maple-hill-manor-bed-and-breakfast/.

10. www.springhillwinery.com/plantation-history.htm.

11. Ibid.

12. www.bitofthebluegrass.com/2010/10/ghosts-in-hallway-at-gratz-park-inn.html.

13. www.youtube.com/watch?v=ClBjLvHf-PA.

14. http://mansionatgriffingate.com/history.html.

15. Brown, Alan. *Haunted Kentucky: Ghosts and Strange Phenomena of the Bluegrass State*. Mechanicsburg, PA: Stackpole Books, 2009, pp. 16–19.

16. www.brownhotel.com/.

17. Ibid.

18. www.seelbachhilton.com/seelbach-experience#history.

19. Ibid.

20. www.christophersbb.com/.

Chapter Three

1. Meyer, Daniel. "Louisville—a Ghost Story." *Back Home in Kentucky Magazine* (2002), pp. 22–24.

2. http://parks.ky.gov/parks/resortparks/jenny-wiley/history.aspx.

3. Starr, Patti. *Ghosthunting Kentucky*. Cincinnati, OH: Clerisy, 2010, pp. 213–222.

4. Pack, Todd. *The Stories of Jenny Wiley: Exploring the History and the Legends*. Franklin, TN: Atom Media, 2013, p. 120.

5. http://parks.ky.gov/parks/historicsites/wickliffe-mounds/history.aspx.

6. Holland, Jeffrey Scott. *Weird Kentucky*. New York: Sterling, 2008, pp. 20–21.

7. http://kentuckyghosts.com/ghost-stories/ghost-bride-of-cumberland-falls.php.

8. www.angelfire.com/tn3/masterdetective2/Old_Mystery1.pdf.

9. www.wvgenweb.org/mason/roster.html.

10. www.wvculture.org/history/journal_wvh/wvh56-5.html.

11. Brown, Alan. *Haunted Kentucky: Ghosts and Strange Phenomena of the Bluegrass State*. Mechanicsburg, PA: Stackpole Books, 2009, pp. 5–7.

12. www.lex18.com/story/30589926/mystery-monday-whos-haunting-fort-harrod.

13. http://parks.ky.gov/findparks/histparks/pb/.

14. http://weekinweird.com/2015/06/10/investigate-perryville-kentucky-where-the-ghosts-of-the-civil-war-haunt-the-blood-stained-battlefields/.

15. www.dailymotion.com/video/x2ah55e_ghost-adventures-s08e11-battle-of-perryville-field-hospital_tech.

16. http://parks.ky.gov/parks/resortparks/natural-bridge/history.aspx.

17. www.nps.gov/maca/index.htm.

18. www.mnn.com/lifestyle/eco-tourism/photos/8-creepiest-places-in-us-national-parks/mammoth-cave.

19. www.prairieghosts.com/mammoth.html.

Chapter Four

1. www.kentuckytourism.com/colville-covered-bridge/3487/.

2. Starr, Patti. *Ghosthunting Kentucky*. Cincinnati, OH: Clerisy, 2010), pp. 28–35.

3. http://virginsheets.blogspot.com/2011/10/my-haunted-hometown-colville-covered.html.

4. http://moviepilot.com/posts/2934099.

5. Holland, Jeffrey Scott. *Weird Kentucky*. New York: Sterling, 2008, p. 171.

6. Ibid., pp. 170–171.

7. https://urbanlegendsofbarren.wordpress.com/2013/10/05/the-legends-of-middle-bridge/.

8. Hauck, Dennis William. *Haunted Places: The National Directory*. New York: Penguin Books, 1996, p. 189.

9. Holland, Jeffrey Scott. *Weird Kentucky*. New York: Sterling, 2008, p. 177.

10. Hauck, Dennis William. *Haunted Places: The National Directory*. New York: Penguin Books, 1996, pp. 186–187.

11. Starr, Patti. *Ghosthunting Kentucky*. Cincinnati, OH: Clerisy, 2010, pp. 163–172.

12. Holland, Jeffrey Scott. *Weird Kentucky*. New York: Sterling, 2008, p. 173.

13. Ibid., p. 174.

Chapter Five

1. www.Prairieghosts.com/hotrod.html.

2. http://blog.pshares.org/index.php/telling-the-stories-of-the-dead-louisvilles-cave-hill-cemetery/.

3. www.prairieghosts.com/hauntky.html.

4. www.prarieghosts.com/bardst.html.

5. http://forgottenusa.com/haunts/KY/6569/Lone%20Oak-%20German%20Cemetery/.

6. http://westkyareatalk.blogspot.com/2012/04/della-barnes-statue-needs-to-be.html.

7. Hauck, Dennis William. *Haunted Places: The National Directory*. New York: Penguin Books, 1996, p. 187.

8. www.thenewsenterprise.com/articles/2003/04/08/news/news05.txt.

9. www.hauntedplaces.org/item/gates-of-hell-grandview-cemetery-kaseys-cemetery/.

Suggested Reading

David Dominé

Ghosts of Old Louisville
Lexington, KY: University Press of Kentucky, 2005, 2017

Haunts of Old Louisville
Lexington, KY: University Press of Kentucky, 2009, 2017

Phantoms of Old Louisville
Lexington, KY: University Press of Kentucky, 2006, 2017

True Ghost Stories and Eerie Legends from America's Most Haunted Neighborhood
CreateSpace, 2014

Dennis William Hauck

The National Directory: Haunted Places
New York: Penguin Books, 1994

**Jason Hawes and Grant Wilson
(with Michael Jan Friedman)**

Ghost Hunting
New York: Pocket Books, 2007

Michael Paul Henson

More Kentucky Ghost Stories
Johnson City, TN: Overmountain, 1996

Jeffrey Scott Holland

Weird Kentucky
New York: Sterling, 2008

Robert W. Parker

Haunted Louisville
Decatur, IL: Whitechapel, 2007

Haunted Louisville 2
Decatur, IL: Whitechapel, 2010

Haunted Louisville 3
Decatur, IL: Whitechapel, 2014

Patti Starr

Ghosthunting Kentucky
Cincinnati, OH: Clerisy, 2010

Dave Thompson

Haunted America FAQ
Montclair, NJ: Backbeat Books, 2015

Lisa Westmoreland-Doherty

Kentucky Spirits Undistilled
Atglen, PA: Schiffer, 2009

Bibliography

Brown, Alan. *Haunted Kentucky: Ghosts and Strange Phenomena of the Bluegrass State*. Mechanicsburg, PA: Stackpole Books, 2009.

Brown, Alan. *Stories from the Haunted South*. Jackson, MS: University Press of Mississippi, 2004.

Hauck, Dennis William. *Haunted Places: The National Directory*. New York, NY: Penguin Books, 1996.

Holland, Jeffrey Scott. *Weird Kentucky*. New York, NY: Sterling, 2008.

Pack, Todd. *The Stories of Jenny Wiley: Exploring the History and the Legends*. Franklin, TN: Atom Media, 2013.

Starr, Patti. *Ghosthunting Kentucky*. Cincinnati, OH: Clerisy, 2010.

Index